The Impact of Taxes on the American Economy

New Directions in Management and Economics

. . . a series of authoritative books for more effective decision-making . . .

other series titles:

The Impact of Taxes
on the American Economy

LESTER C. THUROW

PRAEGER PUBLISHERS

New York · Washington · London

330.973
T 542

PRAEGER PUBLISHERS
111 Fourth Avenue, New York, N.Y. 10003, U.S.A.
5, Cromwell Place, London S.W.7, England

Published in the United States of America in 1971
by Praeger Publishers, Inc.

Library of Congress Catalog Card Number: 70–141363

Printed in the United States of America

Contents

List of Tables and Charts

Introduction

Tax analysis is one of man's oldest intellectual pursuits, since it began not long after the first primitive leader began clubbing tax payments out of his subjects. In the history of economics, the first few thousand years were devoted solely to the analysis of taxation. The interest continues, and modern literature on taxation is almost as extensive as its history is old. This previous effort makes it possible to provide a comprehensive estimate of the quantitative impact of taxes on the American economy, though, unfortunately, these estimates cannot be obtained from a simple compilation of existing materials.

In some cases there is general agreement among economists on the proper modes of analysis and probable effects, but the analysis has been done at widely varying times and upon inconsistent sets of data. Thus many of the estimates of this book are simply a matter of applying existing analysis to reasonably up-to-date and consistent sets of data. Because of data limitations it is not possible to use data from exactly the same years, but most of the data came from the same period. Given probable ranges of error, the remaining inconsistencies are not important.

While there is a wide range of agreement on the impact of taxes, there are areas in which fundamental differences exist as to proper modes of analysis and probable effects. When these differences do exist, they will be pointed out, the various approaches will be outlined, and the range of probable effects indicated. But I will also indicate the mode of analysis and effects that I believe to be correct. It will be these effects that are carried into the final analysis.

There are also areas in which new modes of analysis need to be developed or in which old modes need to be extended. To provide a comprehensive picture of the impact of *all* taxes, I have attempted to provide the necessary analysis, but I will also indicate where such extensions occur so that the reader can maintain a properly skeptical frame of mind.

In terms of reliability and/or consensus of expert opinion, the quality of the estimates obviously differs. Some of the estimates will be generally accepted; others will be controversial. I can only indicate which is which. Hopefully the analysis that accompanies the estimates will help the reader make his own judgments.

At many points in the analysis, numerical calculations are made. Precise numerical calculations are not intended to lend a specious accuracy to results that reflect substantial ignorance on the part of both the author and the economics profession. The numerical results are merely best estimates of midpoints of actual ranges in which true estimates might lie.

Since taxes are government instruments for altering the distribution of economic resources — on the simplest level they are just a method of transferring resources from the private sector to the public sector — the analysis in Chapter 1 must start with the existing distribution of economic resources. Only by looking at the factors, tax and nontax, that produced changes in these distributions is it possible to determine the impact of taxes on the American economy. At the same time they are also the end of the analysis, since these distributions are what taxes produce. Being directly measurable, they are also what is known with the most certainty.

To analyze the impact of taxes on the distributions of economic resources it is necessary to determine how taxes affect the economic decisions and actions of private individuals and firms, discussed in Chapters 2 and 3. The analysis focuses on how taxes cause them to alter their work effort, savings, investment, and other economic plans. Given an understanding of microeconomic effects it is possible to move on in Chapter 4 to the analysis of tax incidence. Once the incidence of taxes is known it is possible to construct hypothetical distributions of how economic resources would be distributed if taxes did not exist. By comparing the actual distribution of economic resources with these hypothetical distributions a picture of how taxes affect the American economy can be constructed.

Two other pieces of information are necessary to fill in the details of the picture. Since taxes and expenditures affect macroeconomic conditions—unemployment, inflation, growth rates, etc.—of the economy and since macroeconomic conditions affect both the quantity and distribution of economic resources, Chapter 5 analyzes the macroeconomic effects of taxes. And since each state or locality has a different structure of taxes in a federal system, there is a wide range of effects around the average effects. Although it is not the purpose of this book to analyze the impact of taxes in each locality, in Chapter 6 some estimates are made of the ranges of effects produced by a federal system.

In analyzing either the impact of taxes upon the distribution of economic resources or looking at the economic literature on taxation, one is struck by the absence of taxes on physical wealth and the absence of economic literature on wealth taxes. Chapter 7 is therefore devoted to analyzing the role and feasibility of wealth taxes.

There remains the problem of passing normative welfare judgments upon the impacts of the tax system. Does it have a good or bad impact? How do we judge whether its impact is good or bad? In Chapter 8 welfare economics is applied to the economics of taxation. The concluding chapter, Chapter 9, develops the policy implications implicit in the rest of the book.

Ideally, an economist would like to have a perfect general equilibrium model of the American economy that could be simulated with and without taxes and expenditures or with different combinations of taxes and expenditures. The model would embody the economic mechanisms by which taxes affect the distribution of real economic welfare. The simulations would generate the hypothetical distributions of economic welfare and the manner in which taxes and expenditures could be used to move the actual distribution toward society's desired distribution. Practically, the data base, the knowledge, and preferences necessary to construct a perfect model that could be simulated over ranges outside of historical experience do not exist and probably never will exist. As a result, this study uses a more disaggregate approach. It attempts to be comprehensive, but it does not attempt to estimate all of the different effects from some common model; different models are used when they seem appropriate and useful.

Since this book will be discussing the impact of both taxes and expenditures rather than of taxes alone it might have been entitled "The Impact of the Public Sector on the American Economy"; in many cases they are so intertwined it is difficult or impossible to separate them. The primary focus of the analysis, however, is on taxes, and the fact is emphasized that we must be willing to tax ourselves if we are to enjoy the benefits of a public sector in the American economy.

Robert Solow and Richard Musgrave provided many helpful comments on an earlier draft, but, as usual, are not responsible for any remaining errors. Joseph Pechman provided the initial impetus for this book although the final product did not head in the directions he intended. Much of the work was financed under a National Science Foundation grant GS-2811.

The Impact of Taxes on the American Economy

1 The Distribution of Economic Resources

In taxation, knowledge of the existing distributions of economic resources are necessary from three vantage points. (1) Tracing the sources of changes in the existing distribution of resources is the primary method of isolating the impact of taxes from the impacts of other economic events. (2) To determine the impact of taxes it is necessary to compare the actual distribution of economic resources with the distributions that would exist in the absence of taxes. (3) Since tax structures are designed to achieve society's desired distribution of economic resources, it is necessary to know the actual distributions in order to determine whether the present tax structure is acceptable or needs to be altered. As a consequence this chapter is devoted to outlining the existing distributions of economic resources. It sets the stage for further analysis.

Existing Vertical Distributions of Income and Wealth

In December, 1962, the latest date for which data are available, the median American family (families are defined to include unrelated individuals) had a net worth (physical wealth) of $7,550, but the mean net worth was three times as high ($22,588) (*see* Table 1-1). As the difference between median and mean suggests, there is a highly skewed dispersion of physical wealth in the United States. Eight percent of the families have negative net worths (their debts are greater than their assets), 55 percent have net worths of less than $10,000, and 79 percent have net worths of less than $25,000. At the other extreme $2\frac{1}{2}$

TABLE 1-1[1]

Net Worth of Consumers Within Specified Groups, December 31, 1962

Group characteristic	All Families	Negative	0– $999	$1,000– 4,999	$5,000– 9,999	$10,000– 24,999	$25,000– 49,999	$50,000– 99,999	$100,000– 199,999	$200,000– 499,999	$500,000– 999,999	$1,000,000 and over	Mean (dollars)	Median (dollars)
All Families	100	8	17	17	14	24	11	5	1	1	(¹)	(¹)	22,588	7,550
1962 Income:														
0–$2,999	100	12	31	16	15	17	7	1	(¹)	(¹)	(¹)	(¹)	8,875	2,760
$3,000–4,999	100	15	22	22	12	17	8	3	(¹)	1	(¹)	(¹)	10,914	3,320
$5,000–7,499	100	7	14	21	17	28	8	4	1	(¹)	(¹)	(¹)	15,112	7,450
$7,500–9,999	100	3	5	19	16	37	14	5	2	(¹)	(¹)	(¹)	21,243	13,450
$10,000–14,999	100	1	3	9	13	34	24	11	4	1	(¹)	(¹)	30,389	20,500
$15,000–24,999	100	(¹)	(¹)	2	8	18	30	26	7	7	1	(¹)	74,329	42,750
$25,000–49,999	100	1	(¹)	(¹)	1	2	7	20	31	30	5	3	267,996	160,000
$50,000–99,999	100	(¹)	(¹)	(¹)	(¹)	(¹)	1	3	13	37	27	20	789,582	470,000
$100,000 and over	100	(¹)	(¹)	(¹)	(¹)	(¹)	(¹)	(¹)	1	4	61	35	1,554,152	875,000
Age of Family Head:														
Under 25	100	33	48	14	5	(¹)	(¹)	(¹)	(¹)	(¹)	(¹)	(¹)	762	270
25–34	100	18	26	25	15	13	3	1	(¹)	(¹)	(¹)	(¹)	7,661	2,080
35–44	100	8	13	18	18	28	8	5	1	1	(¹)	(¹)	19,442	8,000
45–54	100	7	10	19	10	29	16	6	2	1	(¹)	(¹)	25,459	11,950
55–64	100	2	14	10	14	29	16	9	4	2	(¹)	(¹)	34,781	14,950
65 and over	100	2	17	13	17	25	16	6	1	2	1	(¹)	30,718	10,450

Percentage Distribution of Families, by Net Worth

[1]Board of Governors of the Federal Reserve System, "Survey of Financial Characteristics of Consumers," *Federal Reserve Bulletin* (March 1964), p. 291.

percent of the families have net worths in excess of $100,000 and $\frac{1}{2}$ percent have net worths in excess of $500,000. The mean net worth of this latter group is $1,176,281.

Since most individuals possess the skills and knowledge necessary to earn income, physical assets are only part of each individual's wealth. He has human capital as well as physical capital. Human capital can best be measured by capitalizing the income flows that it produces. Given a 10 percent rate of return on human capital,[1] Table 1-2 indicates the distribution of human capital in the American economy. Slightly over 10 percent of the population has human capital of less than $10,000 while 13 percent of the population has human capital in excess of $100,000. Four-tenths of 1 percent of the population has human capital in excess of $250,000.[2]

TABLE 1-2[1]
Distribution   of   Human
Capital in 1962

Human Capital ($)	Percentage
0–9,999	10.4
10,000–19,999	7.6
20,000–29,999	7.6
30,000–39,999	9.1
40,000–49,999	10.1
50,000–59,999	12.1
60,000–69,999	10.6
70,000–79,999	8.0
80,000–99,999	10.8
100,000–149,999	10.5
150,000–249,000	2.5
250,000 and over	0.4

[1]Census Bureau, *Current Population Reports, Consumer Income,* Series P = 60, no. 41 (1962), pp. 50, 69.

The distribution of income (*see* Table 1-3) is a measure of the distribution of wealth, but it is an imperfect measure for several reasons. First, computed incomes exclude unrealized capital gains, earnings from the personal use of assets (homes, cars, etc.), and earnings from financial assets such as life insurance

TABLE 1-3[1]
Distribution of Income in 1962

Income Class ($)	Percentage of Families	Mean Wealth[2]
0–2,999	28	$15,405
3,000–4,999	20	39,564
5,000–7,499	22	67,572
7,500–9,999	15	94,223
10,000–14,999	11	131,439
15,000–24,999	3	212,779
25,000–49,999	1	428,716
50,000–99,999	—[3]	1,022,342
100,000 and over	—	1,827,102

[1]Board of Governors of Federal Reserve System, "Survey of Financial Characteristics," (March, 1964), p. 289.

[2]Calculated on the assumption that human capital earns 10 percent per year in the form of wages and salaries.

[3]Less than $\frac{1}{2}$ of 1 percent.

or pension funds. Second, the assumptions necessary to make income a perfect measure of wealth are probably not fulfilled. Each person does not earn the same rate of return on all human and physical investments, and each factor of production is not paid its marginal product. Thus the distribution of income may not really reflect the actual distribution of wealth. When it is compared with the distributions of human capital and physical capital outlined above, it is obvious that a strange cross-distribution must exist between the two if income were actually a perfect measure of wealth.[3]

The distribution of income is interesting from yet another perspective. The high correlation between income and consumption expenditures means that the existing cross-distributions of net worths by income class (*see* Table 1-1) will be very similar to the nonexistent cross-distributions of net worths by consumption class. Thus, knowing that families with incomes of less than $3,000 have mean net worths of $8,875 and that families with incomes over $100,000 have mean net worths of $1,554,152 allows us to make inferences about the joint distribution of consumption plus physical wealth (*see* Table 1-3).

Since income is an inadequate measure of wealth, the best procedure for determining total wealth is to capitalize the returns from human capital (wages and salaries) and add them to our direct measures of physical wealth. With a 10 percent rate of return, the mean wealth (human plus physical) for different income classes is given in Table 1-3. Wealth increases from $15,405 for those with incomes of $0 to $2,999 to $1,827,102 for individuals with incomes in excess of $100,000.

Existing Distributions of Consumption and Leisure

Private consumption expenditures are much more equally distributed than the distribution of wealth (*see* Table 1-4). Twelve percent of all families have consumption expenditures of less than $2,000 per year, 56 percent have consumption expenditures of less than $7,500 per year, and only 2 percent of the families have consumption expenditures in excess of $15,000 per year. In aggregate, the bottom 35 percent of all families have 15 percent of total consumption and the top 9 percent of the families have 23 percent of total consumption.[4]

Since leisure time is a major consumption good that is left out of the distribution of consumption expenditures, the distribution of leisure time needs to be examined along with the distribution of consumption expenditures (*see* Table 1-5). With every individual being given the equal start of a 24-hour day, the distribution of leisure time is the most equally distributed of all economic goods. Even here, however, there is a reasonably wide dispersion. Eleven percent of the noninstitutional population 14 years of age and above has 112 hours of leisure per week, and 13 percent of the population has less than 65 hours of leisure per week.

Since the distribution of leisure is the inverse of the distribution of work effort, the distribution of leisure provides a way of measuring how much of the dispersion in the distribution of other economic goods (income, etc.) can be explained by the dispersion in work effort. Basically, work effort is much more equally distributed than any of the other economic goods. Most of the dispersion in income and other economic goods must be explained by factors other than the work effort.

TABLE 1-4[1]
Distribution of Nonfarm Families and One-Person Units by Amount of Current Outlay by Income and Family Size, for Age, by One- and Two-Person Units, 1960–61

Income Class After Taxes	All Classes		Current Outlay[2]									
	Number (000)	Percent	Under $1,000	$1,000-1,999	$2,000-2,999	$3,000-3,999	$4,000-4,999	$5,000-7,499	$7,500-9,999	$10,000-14,999	$15,000 and over
			One-Person Unit – All Ages									
Total	8,172	100.0	13.5	32.4	22.8	12.9	9.0	8.0	0.9	0.4	0.1
Under $1,000	1,302	100.0	66.3	26.8	3.9	1.1	1.1	0.9	—	—	—
$1,000–1,999	2,403	100.0	9.6	73.9	12.6	3.2	0.5	0.1	—	—	—
2,000–2,999	1,531	100.0	0.3	28.6	54.0	12.3	2.9	1.8	0.1	—	—
3,000–3,999	1,193	100.0	—	5.8	38.6	35.5	15.1	4.5	0.3	0.3	—
4,000–4,999	831	100.0	0.6	2.1	19.0	26.7	32.7	17.8	0.7	—	0.4
5,000–5,999	369	100.0	—	—	11.3	16.2	31.4	34.3	4.7	2.1	—
6,000–7,499	338	100.0	—	—	3.7	12.6	17.5	58.7	7.6	—	—
7,500–9,999	135	100.0	—	—	3.5	13.8	25.8	45.7	11.3	—	—
10,000–14,999	56	100.0	—	—	8.5	8.2	6.1	36.4	8.5	24.1	8.2
15,000 and over	14	100.0	—	—	—	—	—	—	—	75.8	24.2

Families of Two or More

			0.7	5.4	8.9	11.7	13.8	32.6	16.1	8.3	2.5
Total	43,626	100.0									
Under $1,000	452	100.0	46.9	39.6	5.3	0.9	0.4	4.7	2.2	—	—
$1,000–1,999	2,663	100.0	3.0	64.5	23.0	5.4	2.3	1.2	0.5	—	—
2,000–2,999	4,038	100.0	0.1	10.2	55.8	24.1	6.5	2.4	0.5	0.3	0.1
3,000–3,999	4,814	100.0	—	1.0	15.1	45.8	23.2	12.0	1.5	1.0	0.3
4,000–4,999	6,122	100.0	—	0.3	3.0	19.5	41.8	31.2	3.1	1.0	0.1
5,000–5,999	6,289	100.0	—	—	1.1	6.5	21.7	64.7	4.7	1.0	0.4
6,000–7,499	7,656	100.0	—	—	0.2	1.6	6.1	66.8	21.2	2.9	1.2
7,500–9,999	7,014	100.0	—	—	0.1	0.6	2.1	30.2	51.6	13.7	1.8
10,000–14,999	3,530	100.0	—	—	—	0.5	1.0	7.4	32.1	52.3	6.8
15,000 and over	1,000	100.0	—	—	—	0.2	0.0	1.1	5.5	39.6	1.1
Total	51,798	100	2.7	9.7	11.1	11.9	13.0	28.7	13.7	7.1	2.1

[1]Lenore A. Epstein, "Measuring the Size of the Low Income Population," *Six Papers on the Size Distribution of Wealth and Income*, Lee Soltow, ed. (New York: National Bureau of Economic Research, 1969), p. 190.

[2]Calculated by author, based on data in Tables 1-1, 1-2, 1-3, 1-4, 1-5.

TABLE 1-5[1]
Distribution of Leisure in 1962[2]

Hours Per Week	Percent of All Persons 14 and Above
Less than 65	12.8
65–71	3.9
72–77	62.0
78–97	7.0
98–111	3.2
112	11.1

[1]Bureau of Labor Statistics, *Special Labor Force Report, Labor Force, and Employment, 1960–1962* (May 1963), pp. 25ff.

[2]Calculated on the assumptions that:

a. Eight hours per day are needed for necessary human maintenance activities.

b. Individuals who are not in the labor force because they are either housewives or students work 35–40 hours per week.

c. Government employees work 35–40 hours per week.

Vertical Inequalities

The differing degrees of inequality can be seen by looking at the Lorenz diagrams of leisure, consumption expenditures, human capital, income, income plus physical wealth, and physical wealth (*see* Chart 1-1). Moving from leisure to wealth the distributions become progressively more and more unequal. Lack of data makes it impossible to update Chart 1-1 to a more recent year, but analysis of those distributions for which recent data are available (income, leisure, and human capital) indicates that the distributions have not changed shapes in the intervening years. Note that the distribution of wealth (including human wealth) is much more unequal than the distribution of income. Thus income, as measured, underestimates the inequalities that exist.

Leaving aside the distribution of benefits from public goods and services (government expenditures) for the moment, society must compare its desired distributions with the actual distributions in Chart 1-1 to determine whether its economic system is

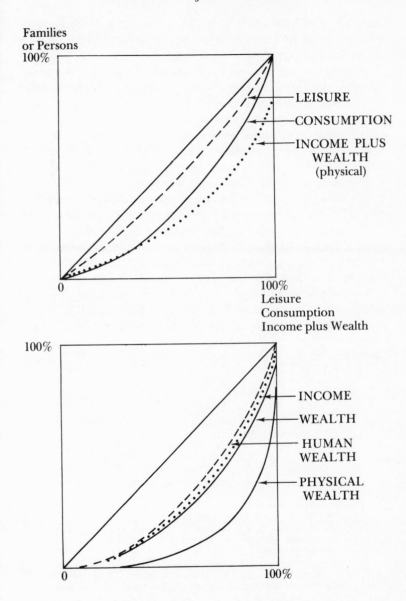

CHART 1–1. Distribution of Economic Resources

vertically equitable or inequitable. However without knowing society's social welfare function, there is no way to say whether these distributions are or are not equitable.

Although each reader must ultimately judge for himself whether the actual distributions are society's desired distributions, there are several pieces of evidence that could lead one to conclude that they are not. The poverty lines set by the federal government in its antipoverty programs is one such indication. Poverty lines are set in terms of income, but they really refer to potential private consumption expenditures. Consequently they can be used as a standard to judge the adequacy of vertical equity at the bottom of the distribution of consumption expenditures. Instead of having a distribution of consumption expenditures under which 8 percent of the families make consumption expenditures of less than $1,490 per year, no family would have consumption expenditures smaller than this amount if poverty had been eliminated (*see* Table 1-6). Basically, eliminating poverty would eliminate the very low levels of consumption and push the whole bottom part of the distribution upward. Radical changes are not made in the distribution of families by consumption class, since families are relatively equally distributed across consumption classes between $2,000 and $5,000. Based on

TABLE 1-6[1]
Distribution of Consumption Expenditures

Consumption Class	Actual (%)	Hypothetical, Based on Elimination of Poverty (%)
0–999	2.7	0
$1,000–1,490	5.1	0
$1,491–2,000	4.6	9.5
$2,000–2,999	11.1	11.7
$3,000–3,999	11.9	13.4
$4,000–4,999	13.0	13.8

[1]Actual figures are from Lenore A. Epstein, "Measuring the Size of the Low Income Population," *Six Papers on the Size Distribution of Wealth and Income*, Lee Soltow, ed. (New York: National Bureau of Economic Research, 1969).

poverty lines, however, society has not achieved its optimum distribution of consumption expenditures.

Questions concerning vertical equity are also raised by the growing gap between nominal tax rates and effective tax rates as incomes rise (*see* Table 1-7). There is a 5.3 percentage-point gap between the nominal tax rates of those with incomes of $600 to $1,000 while there is a 32.5 percentage-point gap between the nominal and effective rates of those with incomes over $1,000,000. It is possible to argue that since tax rates are set in the political arena, any tax structure that emerges reflects society's desired degree of vertical equity. The sharp distinction between nominal and actual rates, however, raises doubts about the actual tax structure being the desired tax structure. If society wants a tax structure that is not very progressive and that is regressive at the top, why did it not legislate a tax structure under which the nominal and actual tax rates are similar if not identical? Why hide actual effective tax rates behind high nominal tax rates? One answer is that society wants a progressive tax structure, but can be sidetracked from its desires by a tax system that appears highly progressive but in fact is not. If the difference between nominal and effective rates of taxation is not designed to confuse the public as to what is really happening, it is hard to think of a justification for playing this complicated game of high nominal rates offset by special provisions. The differences between nominal and effective rates at least create a prima-facie case that the existing tax structure does not reflect society's desires concerning vertical equity, but it may also reflect the problems produced by tax incentives. If incentives are the cause, there is a sharp conflict between society's goals of vertical equity and other public goals to which incentives are directed.

The sharp difference, however, between the degree of equality in the distribution of consumption expenditures (or human capital) and the distribution of physical wealth does raise some question. Does society desire a distribution of wealth that is so much more unequal than the distribution of consumption? Does it want the distribution of consumption plus wealth implied in Tables 1-3 and 1-4? Does it want to have a very unequal

TABLE 1-7[1]
Influence of Various Provisions on Effective Rates of Individual Income
Tax, Taxable Returns, 1964 Act

Total Income Class ($)	Nominal Tax[1] (%)	Reduction Due to			Actual Tax (%)
		Deductions (%)	Capital Gains Provisions (%)	Income Splitting (%)	
600–1,000	5.1	4.4	—	—	0.8
1,000–1,500	7.3	3.6	—	—	3.8
1,500–2,000	8.4	3.1	—	—	5.3
2,000–2,500	9.1	2.9	—	—	6.2
2,500–3,000	9.9	2.7	—	—	7.1
3,000–3,500	10.0	2.7	—	0.1	7.1
3,500–4,000	10.3	2.8	—	0.1	7.2
4,000–4,500	10.6	2.8	—	0.2	7.5
4,500–5,000	11.0	2.9	—	0.3	7.7
5,000–6,000	11.5	3.1	0.1	0.4	7.8
6,000–7,000	12.1	3.2	0.1	0.6	8.1
7,000–8,000	13.3	3.4	0.1	0.8	8.9
8,000–9,000	14.3	3.5	0.1	1.0	9.5
9,000–10,000	15.5	3.7	0.1	1.3	10.3
10,000–11,000	16.5	3.9	0.1	1.6	10.8
11,000–12,000	17.4	4.0	0.2	1.8	11.3
12,000–13,000	18.5	4.2	0.3	2.1	11.9
13,000–14,000	19.4	4.4	0.3	2.3	12.4
14,000–15,000	20.3	4.6	0.3	2.6	12.7
15,000–20,000	22.8	5.2	0.7	3.2	13.6
20,000–25,000	27.5	6.0	1.2	4.6	15.4
25,000–50,000	35.3	7.1	2.1	6.7	19.2
50,000–100,000	47.4	8.8	5.2	7.2	26.1
100,000–150,000	56.6	10.4	11.5	5.5	28.8
150,000–200,000	60.7	10.9	16.3	4.0	29.1
200,000–500,000	64.5	10.9	22.3	2.4	28.6
500,000–1,000,000	67.6	10.0	29.0	0.9	27.3
1,000,000 and over	69.2	8.0	34.1	0.2	26.7
Total	17.8	4.1	0.9	1.7	10.9

[1]Joseph A. Pechman, *Federal Policy*, The Brookings Institution, Washington, D.C., (1966) p. 284.

distribution of economic power? If the nominal income tax rates are used as an indication of how society wants wealth taxed (the reader will remember that the income tax is an indirect tax on wealth), wealth should be much more equally distributed than it is.

To the extent that the poverty program is designed to raise people's incomes, but to raise them through productive employment, the poverty program is an attempt to alter the distribution of human capital. Thus society is presumably saying that it is unsatisfied with the current distribution of human capital and wants to raise each individual's human capital if he is earning an above-poverty income. Assuming a 10 percent rate of return on human capital, society is establishing a human capital poverty line for income. The human capital poverty line is $16,350 for a 1-person family and rises to $54,300 for a family with 7 or more persons (*see* Table 1-8). Thus, eliminating poverty would raise the bottom portion of the existing distribution of human capital.

TABLE 1-8[1]
Human Capital Poverty
Lines in 1967

Persons in Family	Human Capital Poverty Line
1	$16,350
2	$21,150
3	$26,000
4	$33,350
5	$39,300
6	$44,100
7 or More	$54,300

[1]Census Bureau, *Current Population Reports, Consumer Income*, Series P-60, no. 54 (1967), p. 8.

Horizontal Inequalities

Vertical inequalities are examples of errors of omission in the tax system. Taxes are supposed to eliminate them, but they are produced by the private economy. Horizontal inequalities, however, are examples of errors of commission on the part of the tax system. Instead of treating equals equally, the tax system treats equals unequally. Some indication of the horizontal inequalities produced by the tax system can be seen in the dispersion in the federal income tax rates for taxpayers with the same pretax incomes (*see* Table 1-9). Four percent of the taxpayers with incomes of more than $1 million a year pay effective tax rates of less than 5 percent, while 7 percent of those taxpayers with the same incomes pay effective tax rates of 65 to 70 percent. Thus, 28 percent of the taxpayers with adjusted gross incomes of $1½ million a year will end up with less income after taxes than the taxpayers who have adjusted gross incomes of only half as much ($750,000) but who pay no taxes.

The difference between what is and what could be is illustrated by the standard deviations that now exist in the federal personal income tax and the standard deviations that would exist if comprehensive tax reforms, such as those suggested by the Carter Commission for Canada, were adopted in the United States. The standard deviation of effective tax rates would be reduced in all income classes, but the largest reductions would occur for those with large incomes (*see* Table 1-10). The standard deviation in effective tax rates for those with incomes of more than $1 million per year would fall from 17.7 percentage points to 5.3 percentage points.

The income tax can be viewed as a tax on wealth, but horizontal and rank order inequities with respect to wealth are also created by the limited scope of direct wealth taxes. Since these taxes cover some, but not all, types of wealth, different individuals will obviously pay different taxes depending upon the composition of their assets. In a world of perfect markets, shifts in portfolio balance would equalize the private rates of after-taxes so that all assets yielded the same after-tax rate of return regardless of whether they were taxed or not. But, unfortunately, markets are not perfect and do not adjust instantaneously. Thus the limited scope of wealth taxation can lead to horizontal inequities. The man whose wealth is in real estate may end up paying higher taxes than a man whose wealth is in tax-free municipal bonds.

TABLE 1-9[1]

Percentage Distribution of Returns by Effective Tax Rate Classes: Present Law Tax as a Percentage of Amended Taxable Income,[2] by AGI Classes, 1969 Levels

AGI (in thousands of dollars)	Effective Tax Rate Classes													
	0 to 5	5 to 10	10 to 15	15 to 20	20 to 25	25 to 30	30 to 35	35 to 40	40 to 45	45 to 50	50 to 55	55 to 60	60 to 65	65 to 70
0 to 3	[3]68.0	0.5	1.5	6.0	[4]	[4]	[4]	[4]	[4]	[4]	[4]	[4]	[4]	[4]
3 to 5	14.2	2.5	11.0	63.0	[4]	[4]	[4]	[4]	[4]	[4]	[4]	[4]	[4]	[4]
5 to 7	3.6	2.1	22.5	71.5	[4]	[4]	[4]	[4]	[4]	[4]	[4]	[4]	[4]	[4]
7 to 10	0.9	1.1	22.4	70.2	5.3									
10 to 15	0.5	0.8	6.2	85.5	6.7	0.4								
15 to 20	0.5	0.7	4.2	72.2	20.1	2.3								
20 to 50	0.4	0.7	3.9	27.5	48.6	14.6	3.3	0.7	0.2				[5]	[5]
50 to 100	0.3	0.4	1.2	4.9	11.9	22.3	34.5	18.5	4.4	1.3	0.3		[5]	[5]
100 to 500	1.0	0.4	0.5	1.6	14.1	15.5	11.2	15.3	19.4	12.2	5.6	2.6	0.5	[5]
500 to 1,000	1.8	0.6	0.6	0.6	24.6	30.0	4.7	5.0	3.5	2.6	4.9	7.9	12.7	0.8
1,000 and over	4.0	0.2	0.2	0.2	31.0	27.2	5.2	1.8	2.4	4.0	1.8	2.7	12.3	6.9
All Classes	21.5	1.1	10.9	52.7	8.4	2.0	0.9	0.5	0.3	0.2	0.2	0.1	0.1	1.0

[1] Committee on Ways and Means, U.S. House of Representatives, and Committee on Finance, U.S. Senate, "Tax Reform Studies and Proposals," U.S. Treasury Department (Washington, D.C.: Government Printing Office, Feb. 5, 1969), Part 1, p. 80.

[2] Amended taxable income is taxable income after deduction changes plus excluded capital gains, tax-exempt interest, and excess of percentage over cost depletion. Amended taxable income is used to maintain a common base for the effective rate computation under present law and under the reform program.

[3] Nontaxable are 67.6 percent.

[4] The percentages in these effective rate classes are not very meaningful because they reflect present law tax divided by a small amount of amended taxable income under the reform program. Amended taxable income for these taxpayers is much smaller than present law taxable income primarily because of the higher MSD under the reform program.

[5] Less than 0.05 percent.

TABLE 1-10[1]

Average Effective Tax Rates and Standard Deviations Under U.S. and Carter Tax Structures, by Total Income Class, 1966 (percent)

Total Income Class (Dollars)	United States		Carter Commission	
	Mean	Standard Deviation	Mean	Standard Deviation
0–1,500	1.84	3.7	0.40	0.8
1,500–3,000	4.33	4.9	3.14	3.2
3,000–5,000	6.33	5.6	5.86	4.6
5,000–7,000	7.93	5.5	8.25	4.2
7,000–10,000	9.04	4.5	10.32	3.6
10,000–15,000	11.32	4.8	12.98	2.8
15,000–20,000	13.90	6.1	15.88	3.0
20,000–25,000	16.86	7.9	18.67	3.3
25,000–50,000	21.57	9.4	23.41	4.2
50,000–100,000	29.43	10.6	32.04	4.6
100,000–500,000	34.22	13.5	41.87	6.5
500,000–1,000,000	39.84	16.6	48.11	6.5
1,000,000 and over	37.32	17.7	49.57	5.3

[1]Joseph A. Pechman and Benjamin A. Okner, "Simulation of the Carter Commission Tax Proposals for the United States," *National Tax Journal* (March 1969), p. 11.

Public Versus Private Uses of Resources

In addition to altering the distributions of resources among individuals, taxes alter the distribution of resources between the public and private sectors. In 1965 taxes were used to divert 20 percent of a Gross National Product of $684 billion to the provision of public goods and services (*see* Table 1-11). In addition, taxes were used to divert another $37 billion worth of resources from one private individual to another through the vehicle of transfer payments. Within the government sector the provision of public goods and services was divided evenly between the federal government and the state and local governments. On the conventional definitions of savings and investment, the public purchased $114 billion worth of public consumption goods and $23 billion of public investment goods.[5] Within the private sector the division was $432 billion of consumption goods and $115

TABLE 1-11[1]
Public Versus Private Uses of
Resources in 1965 (billions)

Gross National Product	$684
Government Purchases	$137
Investment	$23
Consumption	$114
Federal	$67
State and Local	$70
Private Purchases	$547
Consumption	$432
Investment	$115

[1]Office of Business Economics, *Survey of Current Business* (July 1968). pp. 19, 31, 32.

billion of investment goods. (The distribution of expenditures across the different functions of government is examined in Chapter 3).

Conclusions

Analysis of the distribution of economic resources indicates that there are substantial inequalities in the United States. While $2\frac{1}{2}$ percent of the population has 44 percent of all private physical wealth, 8 percent of the population has negative wealth (their liabilities exceed their assets). Other types of economic resources are not as unequally distributed, but there are substantial inequalities in all distributions. The inequalities are reinforced by the fact that there is substantial stability in individual position on these distributions. The man who is poor remains poor and the man who is rich remains rich.

In a study of incomes of the same families in two successive years, 70 percent with incomes below $3,000 in one year had similarly low incomes in the following year.[6] Of the 30 percent who left this low income group, 40 percent secured incomes between $3,000 and $4,000, 20 percent moved into the $4,000 to $5,000 range, and the remaining 40 percent reached or surpassed $5,000. On the other hand, corresponding groups of families were moving back into the low-income classification. Thus personal mobility does not erase the unequal distribution of economic resources in America. Distributions collected over longer periods of time indicate the same degree of inequality as snapshots taken in any one year. Since the distributions also seem to have been stable since World War II there is no way to dismiss these inequalities.[7] They must be accepted or efforts must be made to modify them.

Since taxes are one of the means of reducing inequalities in the distribution of resources, the merits of the current structure of taxes depends in good part upon the readers views as to the acceptability of these distributions. If they are unacceptable, there is a prima-facie case for changing the structure of taxes.

Notes

1. Gary S. Becker, *Human Capital* (New York: National Bureau of Economic Research, 1964), p. 154.
2. These calculations assume that human capital can be measured in terms of one year's income flow when in reality there is no reason to assume that human capital earns 10 percent each year, even if its overall return is 10 percent.
3. Those with the most physical capital would have the least human capital.
4. This distribution includes the value of consumption items received without expense.
5. This is a brick-and-mortar definition of investment. Expenditures such as those in education are counted as consumption expenditures.
6. *Economic Report to the President* (Washington, D.C.: Council of Economic Advisors, January, 1965), p. 163.
7. The distributions have been stable when measured in relative terms, but resource gaps have been widening when measured in terms of absolute differentials.

2 Supplies of Capital and Labor

Taxes have one of their major influences on the distribution of economic resources through their impact on the supplies of capital and labor. When taxes are levied, individuals may decide to alter their work, savings, and investment patterns. To the extent that they do, taxes induce changes in the economy's potential output (that output level consistent with some unemployment target). Such induced changes in potential output are called the "excess burden" of taxation. The direct burden of taxation is measured by tax collections; the indirect burdens (excess burdens) are measured by differences in the level of output with and without taxes. These excess burdens thus form one of the key elements in estimating the impact of taxes, but their estimating depends upon knowing the impact of taxes on the supply of capital and labor.

What happens to the economy's potential output as taxes change? The answer cannot be determined theoretically. Taxes may reduce potential output (excess burdens are positive) or taxes may increase potential output (excess burdens are negative). The answer depends upon the relative strengths of the income effects of taxes leading to more work, savings, and investment in an effort to recoup the individual's standard of living and the substitution effects of taxes leading to less work, savings, and investment as a result of the lower net rate of return to work, savings, and investment. Since every tax, except the lump-sum tax, has both income and substitution effects, it is impossible to know *a priori* whether taxes will lead to larger or smaller supplies of capital and labor.

The impact of taxes also depends upon how they are levied. If they are levied as user charges to pay for goods and services that are provided publicly, but desired by the user (toll highways), they have no more impact on work, savings, and investment decisions than the price of any other goods or service. If general taxes are viewed in a similar manner as the price that must be paid for desired public services, all taxes would become user charges. Taxes would not effect supplies of capital and labor. There are good reasons, however, why such perceptions are not apt to occur. Individuals view public services as free goods. For each individual there is no perceptible connection between the taxes he pays and the public services he receives, although collectively there is such a connection. As a result the individual does not need to be concerned about reductions in public services when individually he decides to alter his economic decisions to reduce his tax payments.

Public services also alter private decisions by being complementary with, or substitutes for, various types of private goods. If a government dam provides a lake for boating, individuals may work harder to be able to purchase a boat. In this case the public service is complementary with work effort. Taxes to pay for the dam may lead to less work effort, but this negative effect is overwhelmed by the positive effect on work effort provided by the public good. After the boat has been purchased, the lake may have the opposite effect. The individual may work less than he did before the lake was constructed because he enjoys his leisure more. At this point the lake becomes a substitute for private goods and leads to less work effort. Thus the existence of public services can lead to more or less work effort, and at different points in time the same public service can do both.

Government expenditures may affect returns on investment in a similar manner. Public services may be complementary with investment—i.e., raise the gross rate of return on investment. Benefit taxes such as highway and gasoline taxes provide the clearest examples. Trucking firms pay taxes that other industries do not pay (the highway and gasoline taxes), but they receive specific government benefits (highways) in return. Trucking firms have the option of not paying highway taxes and not using the highways. They choose to pay these extra taxes because the benefits outweigh the costs. Other expenditures, such as policy protection, fire protection, and public education, have similar impacts on private gross rates of return on investment expenditures.

Tax impacts also depend upon the degree of money illusion. If workers look only at their take-home earnings when making work decisions and savings decisions, income taxes and payroll taxes are the major taxes influencing these decisions. If they look at their real take-home earnings, these decisions will be indirectly affected by any tax that influences the prices of goods and services. While money illusion may exist in the short run, long-run effects presumably depend upon real rather than money incomes. This presumption is made for a number of reasons. If money illusion did exist, it would be possible to fool all of the people all of the time. If only indirect taxes were levied, people would never know that they were taxed. This proposition is hard to believe.

The Work-Leisure Decision

With both income and substitution effects, neither the direction nor the magnitude of the impacts of taxes on the supply of labor can be determined theoretically. Substitution effects (lower take-home wage rates) lead to less work; income effects (lower incomes) lead to more work. Taxes also permit government expenditures. If individuals think that government expenditures increase their real incomes more than government taxes reduce their real incomes, the income effect may in fact lead to less work rather than more work. In this case the income effect and the substitution effect exert a force in the same direction. Both lead to less work effort.

In reality, the work decision is multidimensional. It is not simply "to work or not to work." Individuals must decide the age at which they will begin work, the age at which they will stop work, their hours of work per week and per year, how intensively they will work, and in what form they would like to receive their pay. All of these decisions may be affected by taxes, but they are also affected by a variety of other factors. Desires to succeed, to be praised, to satisfy oneself, or to acquire economic power are all alternative reward systems that may dominate taxes in making these basic decisions.

To some extent work-leisure decisions are made collectively rather than individually. Our institutional arrangements guarantee that most individuals will begin work when they graduate from high school or college, will stop work at approximately 65 years of age, will work the standard work week and the standard work year, will work with an intensity dependent upon the diligence of their bosses and the speed of the assembly lines, will make occupational and industrial choices based on a broad variety of sociological and economic factors, and will be paid in the form of wages and salaries. As a result, to a large extent their work-leisure decisions are independent of taxes.

Most of the existing literature on work decisions focuses on the decisions of the very rich, managers, the self-employed, and professional workers.[1] These groups are thought to have fewer institutional constraints on their work decisions. The analysis also focuses on the high nominal tax rates of the federal income tax (when most of these studies were done nominal tax rates rose to 90 percent). Analysis indicated that taxes had little impact on work decisions in aggregate (some people worked more, some worked less). Income and substitution effects seemed to balance.

The observed effects were primarily on the method of compensation. Where possible, individuals attempt to receive their income in those forms that are taxed at lower rates—capital gains, deferred compensation, expense accounts, pension plans, etc. There is also some indication that individuals are target savers for their old age. To meet target savings goals in the face of taxes, they work longer and retire later.

At the moment there are several experiments under way to determine the impact of negative income taxes upon the work-leisure decisions of the poorest parts of the population.[2] These programs should lead to less work effort, since the individuals are given higher incomes (and at the same time their marginal tax rates are increased). Both income and substitution effects are adverse to work effort, yet preliminary results seem to indicate that work effort is not reduced.

Ideally, economists would like to know the impact of taxes on the supply of labor. Labor supply functions for the American economy have been estimated, but they typically ignore taxes.[3] This is true with respect to both labor participation functions and hours of work. In both functions, however, there are unexplained trend terms. There is a downward trend in male participation rates, an upward trend in female participation rates, and a downward trend in the number of hours worked per year. These trends probably represent the long-run impact of rising incomes and changing wage rates, but the short-run variability in wages and incomes is too large to find significant correlations between income, wages, and work effort in labor supply functions. If these trend terms do represent income or wage effects, however, they can be used to estimate the impact of taxation on the supply of labor.

In the postwar period male participation rates have been falling while female participation rates have been rising. If these changes were produced by economic conditions, the income effects of rising incomes must dominate the substitution effects of rising wages for males while the reverse is true for females. Other interpretations are possible. Sociological forces rather than economic forces may lead to higher female participation rates. If declining hours of work per year are interpreted economically, the income effect must dominate the substitution effect on hours of work.

Since falling male participation rates and falling hours of work per year are quantitatively more important than rising female participation rates, the net effect is a reduction in work effort. Subtracting increases in the labor force due to population growth from the actual growth in the labor supply, per capita disposable personal income rose 3.5 percent a year in real terms while the labor supply was falling 0.24 percent a year in the 1960's.[4] (This estimate comes from some labor supply functions estimated by the author, but it agrees with the results gotten from most other labor supply functions.)[5]

Labor supply functions thus indicate that the income effects of rising incomes dominate the substitution effects of rising wage rates. With higher incomes and high wage rates, individuals work less, not more. Labor supply functions, however, do not necessarily indicate the reversibility of this phenomenon. Since there are no recent long-run periods of falling incomes and wage rates, no one knows what the corresponding trend terms would look like in labor supply functions fit to such periods.

The most convenient assumption is that of reversibility. Lower income and wage rates are assumed to produce an equivalent increase in work effort. This need not be true, however. There may be a fundamental asymmetry. Lowering taxes may lead to less work effort, while raising taxes does not lead to equivalent increase in work effort. Thus the effect of eliminating taxes may not be the same as the effect of imposing taxes.

If all taxes had been eliminated and the tax reductions had been shared between corporate and personal income in such manner as to leave their income shares unaffected, per capita disposable income would have been 43 percent higher in 1968. Using the estimated relationship between increases in real standards of living and reductions in work effort (every 3.5 percent increase in incomes leads to a 0.24 percent reduction in work effort), the supply of labor would fall by 3.0 percent if all taxes were eliminated and government expenditures were held constant. The reduction is small since Americans do not seem to be taking much of the country's increasing productivity in the form of leisure.

A 3 percent reduction in available labor can be translated into an output reduction by inserting the new smaller labor force into an aggregate production function. Such production functions indicate the precise connections between the supplies of capital and labor and the economy's output. With the production functions used in this analysis a 3.0 percent reduction in labor supplies leads to a 2.5 percent reduction in the Gross National Product. Thus, if taxes were eliminated, output would be reduced 2.5 percent. If the converse were true, imposing taxes would increase the labor supply by 3.0 percent and lead to a 2.5 percent increase in output. As a result the "excess burden" of taxes is negative with respect to supplies of labor. (Although one particular production function is used to generate these estimates, other production functions lead to similar results.)

The Savings-Consumption Decision

Supplies of capital can be viewed from the perspective of both savings and investment decisions. Since they are often made by two different people, both decisions need to be investigated to determine the impact of taxes. This is also necessary since certain types of investment (residential housing) do not contribute to potential output in the same manner as normal business investment in plant and equipment.

Since government "saves" some of its revenue and invests them in public investment projects, just as corporations both save and invest,[7] tax impact on savings depends upon the marginal savings propensity of private individuals and businesses and the marginal savings propensities of governments. Using a bricks and mortar definition of investment, corresponding to a definition used in the private sector, 20 percent of general government revenues were devoted to investment by all levels of government in 1966–1967.[8] If the definition is expanded to include investment in human capital, the percentage devoted to investment rises to 37 percent when all education expenditures are counted as investment expenditures, and to 41 percent when all health and hospital expenditures are added. If these average propensities are also marginal propensities, taxes increase or decrease total savings depending upon whether marginal private savings propensities are greater or less than 20 percent or 41 percent.

For the private economy, the average savings propensity was 18 percent in 1968 under the narrow definition of savings and 23 percent under the wide definition that includes private education and health expenditures.[9] Under the narrow definition of savings, persons account for one-third of total private savings and institutions account for the remaining two-thirds.

With either a proportional or progressive tax system, the average savings propensity out of taxable income will be higher than the private economy's average savings propensity. If all of our taxes (federal, state, and local) are approximately equivalent to a proportional tax system (some evidence points in this direction),[10] each taxpayer paid taxes amounting to 37 percent of his income. Given such a tax system and the observed savings propensities across income classes, the average savings propensity of taxpayers (personal plus corporate) is 27 percent under the narrow definition of savings and 35 percent under the wide definition of savings.[11] With a public savings propensity of 20 percent and a private savings propensity of 27 percent, a proportional tax system with a 37 percent tax rate reduces savings by 3 percentage points ($[0.20Y - 0.27Y)(0.37) = -0.03Y]$, where Y = income). On the wide definition of savings, savings rises by 5 percentage points ($[(0.41Y - 0.27Y)(0.37)] = 0.05Y$). Thus, depending upon the definition of investment, the American tax system reduces savings by 3 percentage points, or increases savings by 5 percentage points.

A 3 percentage point reduction in the savings rate would lead to slower growth in the capital stock while a 5 percentage point increase would lead to faster growth in the capital stock. If the previous procedure of inserting the alternative supplies of capital into an aggregate production function is followed, the changes in savings can be translated into changes in output. If taxes had not been collected, potential output would have been 2 percent higher than it was under the first definition of savings and 3 percent lower than it was under the second definition of savings.[12]

Different taxes, however, have different impacts on savings. From 1960 to 1968, the average (and marginal) propensity to save out of disposable personal income was 6 percent under the narrow definition of savings and 12 percent under the wide definition of savings.[13] Consequently, consumption taxes (sales, etc.) and income taxes would reduce private savings by 6 cents, or 12 cents per dollar of revenue collected. Because of public savings out of each dollar, net savings would rise by 14 cents (0.20–0.06) or 29 cents (0.41–0.12).

The savings impact of the corporation income tax depends upon its incidence. If the tax is paid by capitalists, the reduction in private savings is larger and the net increase in total savings is smaller for the corporation income tax than for other taxes.

Given a dividend payout ratio of 47 percent (the 1960 to 1968 average) the marginal savings propensity for corporations is 53 percent. Since dividends go to stockholders with above-average savings propensities, 12.9 percent of dividends are saved on the narrow definition of savings.[14] Thus the average savings propensity for corporate income is 34 percent on the narrow definition of savings and 37 percent on the wide definition. As a result, total savings out of these dollars fall by 14 cents $(0.20 - 0.34)$ on the narrow definition of public investment and rise by 4 cents $(0.41 - 0.37)$ on the wide definition.

If 50 percent of the corporation income tax is shifted forward onto the consumer, every dollar in corporation taxes reduced private savings by 20 cents $((1/2) (0.34) + (1/2) (0.6))$ or 23 cents. Thus there is no change in savings on the narrow definition and an increase in savings of 18 cents on the wide definition. If corporation income taxes are 100 percent shifted forward onto the consumer, their impact is similar to that of consumption taxes.

Social Security taxes have a different character. First, they are forced savings that an individual must make. Being forced, they may have impacts on his other savings plans. Second, the Social Security system also pays benefits. Income is taxed from one group and given to another group. Viewed solely as an income transfer system, income is taken away from individuals with an average savings propensity of 6.6 percent and given to individuals with an average savings propensity of 2.4 percent.[15] Thus, in a year in which the expenditures of the Social Security system equal its revenues, the system reduces private savings by 4.2 cents for every dollar transferred.

Social Security taxes may, however, affect the savings rates of those paying taxes. In noncontributory systems, government pension plans guarantee future consumption and thus reduce the need for private savings to meet future consumption needs. Since the Social Security system is partially noncontributory (each individual gets out more than his contributions plus interest payments on these contributions), there may be some consequent reduction in personal savings (voluntary plus compulsory). If the rates of interest on public and private savings

were identical and the plan was completely financed by the
individual himself, the Social Security system might not affect
savings at all. Social Security taxes would be counterbalanced
by reductions in private savings to yield the same future stream
of income. Alternatively, the taxpayer may find that compulsory
savings fall short of his own targets for one type of savings (for
illness) while exceeding it for another (such as old age). Unless
savings for various purposes can be readily substituted for each
other, compulsory savings may force him to increase his total
savings. Thus theoretical arguments can be advanced for
increases or reductions in private savings of those paying Social
Security taxes.

Empirically there is almost no information on the impact of
the Social Security system on private savings, but there is some
information on the impact of private *compulsory* pension plans.[16]
Private compulsory savings plans seem to result in almost 1-to-1
increases in private savings. In addition, they also seem to stimu-
late individuals to save more out of their disposable incomes. In
one sample other types of private savings rose 0.5 percent for
those who had compulsory pension plans.

Because there has been an increase in voluntary personal
savings since the introduction of the Social Security system, the
same findings may be valid for the Social Security system. When
Social Security taxes are added to voluntary personal savings,
the savings rate has risen from 5.3 percent in 1929 to 14.0 percent
in 1968,[17] but most of this increase has been offset by transferring these savings to beneficiaries with low savings propensities.
Net savings only rose from 5.3 percent to 6.5 percent. These
results may have occurred for other reasons, but surface
evidence does not contradict the findings concerning private
compulsory pension plans.

The impact of property taxes, like corporation income taxes,
depends upon the ultimate incidence of the tax (see below). If
the tax is on the users of the property, the tax would have an
impact on savings very similar to that of consumption taxes. It
would simply be an indirect consumption tax. If the incidence
of the tax is upon property owners, however, the tax will have
a much larger impact on private savings since property owner-

ship is concentrated among those with high savings propensities. Private savings rates are 12 percent or 24 percent, depending upon the definition of savings, for property owners.[18] Thus every dollar of property taxes collected from property owners increases net savings by 8 cents $(0.20-0.12)$ or 17 cents $(0.41-0.24)$.

Property taxes prove to have the same impact on savings as federal income taxes if the incidence of the tax is on property owners. The concentration of property ownership is high enough to produce an effect equal to the concentration of income plus the progressivity of the federal income tax.

Impact on Investment Decisions

In addition to affecting the potential supply of capital goods through their impact on savings, taxes can also affect the demand for capital goods. Net changes in investment are brought about by altering the private (after-tax) rate of return on investment projects. (The macroeconomic effects of taxes also influence the shape and position of the demand curve for capital goods, but these effects are being ignored in this chapter.) With lower rates of return, firms and individuals invest less; with higher rates of return, they invest more.

If a 50 percent corporation income tax with interest deductibility is introduced, the market rate of return is 10 percent, and the investor is using his own funds, the required pretax rate of return must rise from 10 percent to 20 percent to hold the after-tax rate of return constant at 10 percent. To the extent that the investor is using borrowed funds, the necessary increase in the pretax rate of return would be reduced with interest deductibility. If the marginal efficiency of investment schedule (the demand curve) is inelastic, only a small reduction in investment need occur to bring about the necessary increase in the pretax rate of return. If the schedule is elastic, however, large reduction would be necessary. Thus, one part of the empirical problem is to determine the actual elasticity of the marginal efficiency of investment schedules.

The investment impacts of taxation can be most directly measured in econometric investment functions. This is an area with an enormous literature, but the additional investment in plant and equipment produced by a 1 percentage point reduction in the effective corporate income tax rate (a tax revenue loss of $1.3 billion) is given in Table 2-1 for several recent investment functions. The results range from a maximum increase of $0.8 billion in Okun's investment function to a negligible impact in the Brookings and Eisner investment functions. The six functions have an average impact of $0.4 billion with 4 of the 7 functions yielding values close to the average.

Since the effective corporation income tax rate in 1968 was 31 percent of net cash flow, each of the values in Table 2-1 must be multiplied by 31 to determine the total impact of corporation income taxes on corporation investment.[19] Thus the average impact of eliminating the corporate income tax is substantial (it produces a $14 billion increase in investment) even though the impact of each 1 percentage point reduction in taxes is relatively small. For comparison, 1968 investment in plant and equipment was $76 billion in 1958 dollars.

Using the average value in Table 2-1 as a guide, investment expenditures were relatively inelastic with respect to corporate income taxes. Each 1 percent reduction in corporate income taxes lead to a 0.2 percent increase in investment. Based on this elasticity and the aggregate production function used in the previous estimates, corporate taxes reduced investment and led to a 3 percent reduction in potential output.[20] (This reduction cannot be added to the reduction calculated in Section III since it is merely the opposite side of the same coin. In one case savings desires limit investment, and in the other case investment desires limit savings.)

The relatively low elasticities occur since the accelerator process causes most investment. In a growing economy the marginal efficiency of capital schedule moves to the right, and this leads to the need for investment to meet the needs of a growing economy. Movements of the marginal efficiency of investment schedule rather than movements along it control most investment. Consequently, taxes have a smaller impact on investment than might be supposed.

If the corporation income tax were eliminated by eliminating

TABLE 2-1

Tax Impacts on Investment in Plant and Equipment

Investment Function	Extra Investment Produced by 1% Cut in Effective Corporation Income Tax Rate (billions $1958)
Jorgenson[1]	0.4
Thurow[2]	0.5
Okun[3]	0.8
Brookings[4]	0.0[8]
Kuh[5]	0.4
Klein[6]	0.3
Eisner[7]	0.0[8]

[1]Robert E. Hall and Dale W. Jorgenson, "Tax Policy and Investment Behavior," *American Economic Review* (June 1967), pp. 406, 412. Calculated on the basis of allowing first-year writeoff of investment expenditures.

[2]Lester C. Thurow, "A Neo-Classical Disequilibrium Investment Function," *Review of Economics and Statistics* (November 1969), p. 431.

[3]Arthur M. Okun, "Measuring the Impact of the 1964 Tax Reduction," in Walter W. Heller, *Perspective on Economic Growth* (New York: Random House, 1968), p. 44.

[4]Gary Fromm and Paul Taubman, *Policy Simulations with an Econometric Model* (Washington, D.C.: The Brookings Institution, 1968), p.132.

[5]Edwin Kuh, *Capital Stock Growth: A Microeconometric Approach* (Amsterdam, 1963), p. 229.

[6]Michael K. Evans and Lawrence R. Klein, *The Wharton Econometric Forecasting Model* (University of Pennsylvania: Economic Research Unit, 1967), p. 62.

[7]Robert Eisner, "A Permanent Income Theory for Investment," *American Economic Review* (June 1967), pp. 377, 386.

[8]Less than $0.1 billion.

corporations and taxing all income at personal income tax rates, the effect would be much smaller. The effective tax rate on corporation earnings would in fact rise from 31 percent to 35 percent.[21] From this vantage point the corporation income tax can be viewed as a method to reduce personal income tax payments of wealthy stockholders. Thus the corporation income tax may increase investment rather than reduce it if the alternative is personal income taxes.

Impact on Technique of Production

In addition to affecting the level of investment, taxes may alter the distribution of expenditures across different types of investment. Since different types of investment may not be taxed at the same rate, the after-tax distribution of returns may differ from the pretax distribution of returns. To bring after-tax rates of return into equilibrium may require a different distribution of investment expenditures than those necessary to bring pretax rates of return into equality. If two investments each earn 10 percent, the introduction of a tax of 50 percent on one type of investment and 75 percent on another type of investment will require the pretax rates of return to rise to 20 percent and 40 percent respectively to hold posttax rates of return constant. The costs of such distortions were estimated to be $587 million annually between 1953 and 1959 (*see* Table 2-2).

The present tax system also biases investment decisions toward physical investment and away from human capital investments that must be made by the individual. Firms or individuals can depreciate physical investment expenditures to reduce taxable income and firms can expense human capital investment expenditures, but individuals cannot expense or depreciate their own human capital investments. Consequently, the effective tax rate on individual human capital investments is higher than the effective tax rate on physical investment or business investments in training. The exact difference depends upon the rate of return on the investment, the length of life of the asset, and the tax rate. But an individual facing a 50 percent tax rate and trying to decide whether to invest in human capital or a machine, both grossing 20 percent per year and lasting 10 years, will find that the effective tax rate on the net earnings of the human capital investment is 100 percent and that it is only 50 percent on the machine.

Since the entire human capital investment can be deducted in the year in which it is made, a firm facing the same choice could find that the effective tax rate on the human capital investment was actually negative. If it were faced with the same tax rates and had an 8 percent discount rate, the present value of the current deduction from taxable income would exceed the present value of future tax payments owed and the effective tax rate would be − 0.24 percent. Thus the tax bias toward physical investment and toward human capital investments that are undertaken in a business is substantial. The actual distortion that this makes in investment decisions depends upon the elasticity of the different investment schedules.

In reality, however, businesses and individuals do not face the same tax rate. Since corporations undertake most physical investments and most training investments, the effective tax rate (personal plus corporate) for corporate investments is 32 percent versus 14 percent for the average individual (based on effective tax rate on personal income in 1968). Thus the corporate tax advantage and the biases it produces may be offset

TABLE 2-2[1]
Effects on the Use of Capital of Taxes on Corporate Profits and Property, 1953–59 Average

	Taxes as a Percentage of Income from Capital	Costs of Distortion
Total	37	$587 million
Farms, Forestry, and Fisheries	17	$149 million
Mining	30	$17 million
Contract Construction	36	([2])
Manufacturing	47	$241 million
Trade	32	$15 million
Real Estate	28	$81 million
Transportation	46	$14 million
Communication and Utilities	51	$60 million
Services	34	$11 million

[1]Leonard Gerson Rosenberg, "Taxation of Income from Capital, by Industry Group," in Arnold C. Harberger and Martin J. Bailery eds., *The Taxation of Income from Capital* (Washington, D.C.: The Brookings Institution, 1969), p. 123.

[2]Less than 0.5.

by the higher tax rate on corporate investment income. In 1959 the gross rate of return on a college education and on corporate manufacturing investment after payment of the corporation income taxes, but before the payment of personal income taxes were 10 percent and 22 percent respectively.[22] Given a before tax divident payout ratio of 24 percent and a 35 percent tax rate for the average capitalist, the gross return on manufacturing investment was 20.2 percent after payment of personal taxes. The rate of return on the average individual's investment in human capital was 8.6 percent after payment of personal taxes. Thus, the gross returns to physical capital were almost twice the gross returns to a college education. If the rates of depreciation are similar for physical capital and for a college education, net returns are in the same relationship to each other.

Viewed socially, the differences are even larger than when viewed from the point of view of the individual. Society's monetary returns are governed by the before-tax rates of return and not the after-tax rates of return. From society's viewpoint the social gross returns on physical investment in manufacturing are 28 percent (the gross rate of return before corporate plus personal taxes) and only 10 percent on a college education. Viewed as a simple economic good, there is consequently too much invested in a college education and too little investment in manufacturing physical capital.

(This seeming disequilibrium and misallocation of investment resources may be explained by the nonmonetary returns and consumption benefits of education. Individuals may place a value high enough on these returns to make up the 18 percentage points difference in the observed monetary rates of return. Thus these economic calculations do not necessarily indicate that there is too much education.)

There are three other major routes by which taxes can impinge on the choice of production techniques. (1) Different taxes on the earnings of capital and labor may change the relative prices of capital and labor and thus the optimum capital-labor ratio. (2) Special provision in the tax laws may lower (or raise) the relative price of some particular input and lead to a greater use of this input than would be called for if all industries were taxed equally. (3) Some public goods are complementary inputs in the production process (roads, etc.). If benefit taxes are not collected for these free services, production processes will be biased to utilize too many public goods because they seem like free goods to the producer although they are not free goods to society.

The answer to the first question must wait until Chapter 7 since some further analysis of tax incidence is necessary, but the next two questions raise interesting problems here. Those minerals that are subject to percentage depletion and special expensing provisions might be good examples of cases in which tax-induced changes in relative prices lead to overutilization of some particular productive inputs. Agria calculates that depletion allowances and expensing privileges create a tax advantage that makes it profitable to invest $1.5 in searching for oil, $2.3 in searching for coal, and $2.1 in searching for iron for every $1 invested in prospects that would earn the same flow of earnings but do not have these special tax provisions.[23]

Although there might be much more invested in searching for these minerals than there would be if all industries were treated equally under the tax laws, it is not possible to jump to the conclusion that these minerals are overutilized. Other market conditions, such as government regulations and monopolies, may offset the impact of tax laws. Oil provides the most interesting example since it is subject to a wide variety of other forces and since it has been the most extensively investigated. In addition to favorable tax laws, oil is produced under state regulation of production in the largest producing areas, oil import quotas, and oligopoly conditions. While the tax laws work to increase the supply of oil, all of these latter conditions work to restrict the supply of oil. To determine whether oil was over or under utilized it is necessary to know which of these sets of effects dominates.

With the world price of oil substantially lower than the American price (the price differential is approximately $1 per barrel at east coast points of entry),[24] the net effect of all government incentives or disincentives is to raise the U.S. price of oil above what it would be in the absence of all special government attention. Thus tax laws designed to increase the supply of oil and lower its prices cannot lead to overutilization of oil. They simply lead to a misallocation of resources through overinvestment in U.S. oil production. This overinvestment is then compounded by quotas that yield artificial high prices and more domestic investment.

Taxes can also create major distortions in labor services such as that created by a special tax in kind — conscription. Conscription means that the Defense Department can obtain labor for less than its economic price. The result is to bias the choice of production techniques within the Defense Department toward low capital-labor ratios. In the Defense Department's fighting activities this bias is offset by a desire to prevent the loss of human life, but the bias probably leads to underutilization of capital in the military's housekeeping and supply functions. There are no good estimates, however, of the overutilization of labor. Obtaining such an estimate would require a detailed investigation of the Defense Department's production techniques. In any case, it might be excused as a necessary cost of having a democratic army.

The impact of social insurance taxes upon general labor supplies is discussed in Chapter 7, but social insurance taxes are sometimes charged with biasing business choices toward skilled rather than unskilled labor, since the tax rate on high-income employees is less than the tax rate on low-income employees. Assuming that individuals are paid their marginal products, such a situation cannot arise since the burden of the tax is upon the individual and not the employer. Social insurance taxes affect the relative take-home prices of skilled and unskilled labor, but they do not affect the relative prices that businesses face when deciding what types of labor to hire.[25]

Complementary public factors of production are probably just as important as tax differences in producing production biases. The major area of bias is probably the transportation industry although there are continuous disputes as to which mode is relatively favored. Airline users do not completely pay for the costs of airports and although road users pay for roads, truckers *may* not pay their fair share of the total costs. Even if truckers *do* pay their share of road construction and mainten-ance costs there is still the problem of right-of-way taxation. Railroad costs include the taxes levied upon their right of way while truck costs do not. On the other hand, railroads were initially given these rights of way on very favorable terms. They now own valuable pieces of property while truckers are only allowed to use valuable pieces of property. Since for many goods the cross-price elasticity of demand is high, substantial dis-tortions may be introduced into the American transportation network because of taxes, or the lack of them, but sorting out this dispute is a book in its own right.

Government research expenditures are another example of complimentary public services. Because private individuals and businesses are unable to capture all of the benefits of research, especially basic research, and because risks are high, the govern-ment devotes a major fraction of its revenue to research. In 1968 the government spent 5.6 percent of its revenue on research and development while the private sector spent only 1.6 percent of its disposable income.[26] (The Federal government actually spent 8.8 percent of its income for research and development). Most of this research benefits particular firms or individuals. To the extent that they are not taxed to support it, production is biased toward research-intensive industries. Their private costs do not reflect the social costs of producing the research knowledge that they use.

Industries that create air, land, or water pollution are also favored in our tax system. They are allowed to pollute without having to pay the benefit taxes necessary to clean up their pollu-tion. Thus their costs are lower because they are given a free public good, the right to pollute. Depending upon the price elasticity of demand for different products creating pollution, the distortions in production decisions may be large or small. Since most price elasticities are low, the distortions are probably small but the lack of benefit taxes means that the inputs into the production process do not have to include pollution controls. Thus the real distortion occurs in public goods. Society does not enjoy as much clean air, land, and water as it would if every industry were paying the full costs of its production process. It is difficult to place a value on the benefits of clean air, land, and water, but they are obviously substantial.

Taxes may also cause changes in an investor's willingness to undertake risk. Based on some early work of Musgrave and Domar, proportional income taxes were believed to increase the willingness to undertake risky investments.[27] In a tax system where loss offsets are provided, this result occurs since the government tax system reduced the private risk of any investment by sharing in any loss. With after-tax income decreasing and private risk decreasing, investments are made in projects with higher social risks and with higher expected rates of return.

These theoretical conclusions proved to rest on some strong assumptions.[28] First, there must be a riskless asset. This is generally assumed to be money, but with uncertain prices money is not a riskless asset. Second, the conclusions are implicitly based on the assumption that individuals become more risk averse as they grow wealthier. Rich men should have less absolute risk aversion since expected losses will not be as large in relation to their wealth or income as they would be for the poor, but they may have more relative risk aversion in that they are less willing to risk a given proportion of their assets. The conclusions also depend upon investors having a particular quadratic utility function where the standard deviation of the expected return can serve as an adequate measure of risk. Different utility functions lead to different results and require different measures of risk. Consequently there is no theoretical method to determine the impact of income taxes on the riskiness of the investment portfolios that individuals hold.

Empirical analysis of the problem indicates that income taxes may push the wealthy toward more risky investments to maintain their income levels.[29] This analysis reflects several factors however. With lower rates of taxation on realized capital gains than on regular income and no taxes on unrealized capital gains, the effect may just indicate that income from capital pays a lower tax rate than other types of income. Income taxes, if they were actually collected, might reduce risk-taking. No one knows.

Conclusions

Taxes do not seem to have a large impact on the economy's potential output through their impact on the supplies of capital and labor. If public investment does not contribute to economic output, the positive effects of taxes on labor supplies are approximately counterbalanced by the negative effects on capital supplies. The higher labor supply brought about by taxes would raise output 2.5 percent, and the lower capital supply brought about by taxes would lower output 2 to 3 percent. If public investment makes the same contribution to economic output as private investment, then both supply affects work in the same direction, and potential output is approximately 6 percent higher as a result of taxes.[30]

Notes

1. George Break, "Income Taxes and Incentives to Work," *American Economic Review* (September 1957); Thomas Henry Sanders, *Effects of Taxation on Executives* (Cambridge, Mass.: Harvard University Press, 1951).
2. The Institute for Poverty Analysis at the University of Wisconsin and Institute for Mathematics at Princeton, New Jersey, are conducting a variety of negative income tax experiments.
3. For an exception, see Marvin Kosters, "Effects of an Income Tax on Labor Supply," in Arnold C. Harberger and Martin J. Bailey, eds., *The Taxation of Income from Capital* (Washington, D.C.: The Brookings Institution, 1969), p. 301.
4. Calculated on the basis of labor participation functions and hours of work equations given in Lester C. Thurow, "A Fiscal Policy Model of the United States," *Survey of Current Business* (June 1969) (Washington, D.C.: Government Printing Office), pp. 58, 60.
5. Empirically, these estimates are very similar to those of Kosters, *op. cit.*
6. Calculated on the basis of the production function given in Thurow, *op. cit.*
7. The traditional definition of savings (revenue minus expenditures) is meaningful only from the point of view of macroeconomics and as measured as the amount of public savings that is available from private investment.
8. U.S. Bureau of the Census, *Government Finances in 1966–67*, p. 40.
9. Office of Business Economics, *Survey of Current Business* (July 1969).
10. *See* Tax Foundation, *Tax Burdens and Benefits of Government Expenditures by Income Class, 1961 and 1965* (New York: 1967).
11. Calculated from the savings propensities for different income classes, Bureau of Labor Statistics, *Consumer Expenditures and Income, Total United States, Urban and Rural, 1961–64*, Report no. 237–38 (July, 1964), p. 11.
12. Calculated on the basis of the production function given in Thurow, *op. cit.*
13. Office of Business Economics, *Survey of Current Business* (July 1968); *The National Income and Product Accounts of the United States, 1929–1965*, p. 2.

14. Based on the distribution of stock ownership in *Federal Reserve Bulletin* (March 1964), and distribution of savings propensities in Bureau of Labor Statistics, *Consumer Expenditures and Income. . . .*, p. 304.

15. Based on savings propensities in Bureau of Labor Statistics, *Consumer Expenditures and Income. . . .*, p. 304.

16. Phillip Cagan, *The Effect of Pension Plans on Aggregate Savings: Evidence from a Sample Survey* (National Bureau of Economic Research, 1965).

17. Office of Business Economics, *Survey of Current Business* (July 1968); *National Income and Product Accounts. . . .*, p. 19.

18. Based on the distribution of property ownership, *Federal Reserve Bulletin* (March 1964), and distribution of savings propensities in Bureau of Labor Statistics, *Consumer Expenditures and Income. . . .*

19. Office of Business Economics, *Survey of Current Business* (July 1969).

20. Calculated on the basis of the production function given in Thurow, *op. cit.*

21. Calculated on the basis of the distribution of stock ownership given in the *Federal Reserve Bulletin* (March 1964), and the distribution of income tax rates given in Joseph A. Pechman, *Federal Tax Policy* (Washington, D.C.: The Brookings Institution, 1966), p. 284.

22. Giora Hannoch, "An Economic Analysis of Earnings and Schooling," *Journal of Human Resources* (Summer 1967), p. 322.

23. Susan R. Agria, "Special Tax Treatment of Mineral Industries," in Harberger and Bailey, *op. cit.*, p. 99.

24. Special American tax provisions for oil do not have a substantial impact on the world price of oil.

25. Since private returns are affected, the tax may influence the supply of unskilled and skilled workers, but it will not influence the demand for them.

26. U.S. Senate, Hearings Committee on Labor and Public Welfare, *National Science Foundation Authorization, 1970*, p. 161.

27. Evsey D. Domar and R. A. Musgrave, "Proportional Income Taxation and Risk Taking," *Quarterly Journal of Economics* (May 1944).

28. Martin S. Feldstein, "The Effects of Taxation on Risk Taking," Harvard Institute of Economic Research, Discussion Paper no. 26 (May 1968).

29. John Keith Butters, *Effects of Taxation on Investment by Individuals* (Cambridge, Mass.: Harvard University Press, 1953).

30. This calculation is based on the wide definition of savings.

3 The Demand for Goods and Services

Not only do taxes influence the supplies of goods and services; they are also a major determinant of the demand for goods and services. When taxes alter income and/or prices, demands for goods and services change. Since the structure of demand ultimately influences incomes and the distribution of economic resources, tax-induced changes in demand must be isolated before it is possible to determine the impact of taxes on the distribution of economic resources. This chapter seeks to isolate the impact of taxes upon the demand for goods and services.

Public Goods and Services

Taxes directly alter the demand for goods and services by permitting government expenditures. In 1968 government expenditures amounted to $271 billion out of a Gross National Product of $866 billion. To permit such expenditures $264 billion was collected in tax revenue. The division of these expenditures among the different functions of government is given in Table 3-1. National defense expenditures are larger than those for any other purpose but expenditures on health, education, and welfare total $106 billion. Since the functional distribution of expenditures for governments differs significantly from that of private individuals (*see* Table 3-1), taxes have a substantial direct impact on the demand for goods and services. The demand for products used in government expenditures rises; the demand for products used in private expenditures falls.

43

Table 3-1[1]
Government Expenditures, by Function, 1968 (billions)

Government Total	$271	Private Total[2]	$622
National Defense	81	Investment	126
Space Research and Technology	5	Plant and Equipment	89
General Government	29	Residential Structures	30
International Affairs	3	Change in Inventories	7
Education	45	Personal Consumption	
Health	13	Expenditures	537
Labor	1	Food and Tobacco	125
Welfare	48	Clothing and Accessories	55
Civilian Safety	7	Personal Care	9
Veterans Benefits	8	Housing	77
Agriculture	8	Household Operations	76
Natural Resources	5	Medical Care	39
Commerce	1	Personal Business	30
Transportation	16	Transportation	72
Housing	1	Recreation	34
Public Utilities	1	Education	8
		Religious and Welfare	8
		Foreign Travel and Other	4

[1]U.S. Department of Commerce, *Survey of Current Business* (July 1969), pp. 23, 34.

[2]Government expenditures plus private expenditures do not equal total expenditures because some government expenditures are transfer payments.

Using input-output techniques it is possible to determine what proportion of the demand in different industries is produced by government and what proportion is produced by the private sector of the economy. Since government's demands represent 23 percent of total demands, industries (and the people who work in them) with more than 23 percent of their demands emanating from government expenditures are favored by public expenditures while those with less than 23 percent of their demands emanating from government expenditures are at a disadvantage. Table 3-2 indicates a representative sample of some of the industries aided and hurt. The range is from ordinance with 90 percent of its demands coming from government to apparel with 2 percent of its demands coming from government.

In addition taxes are frequently used to achieve public objectives directly rather than indirectly through expenditures.

TABLE 3-2[1]
Total Direct and Indirect Output Attributable
to Public and Private Sectors

Industry	Public	Private
Nonferrous Metal Ores Mining	38%	62%
New Construction	30%	70%
Ordinance	90%	10%
Food and Kindred Products	3%	97%
Apparel	2%	98%
Chemicals	14%	86%
Glass and Glass Products	12%	88%
Metal Working Machinery	13%	87%
Motor Vehicles	6%	94%
Wholesale and Retail Trade	5%	95%
Hotels	6%	94%

[1]U.S. Department of Commerce, *Survey of Current Business* (November 1969), p. 21.

Instead of levying taxes and conducting expenditures programs, inducements are provided to encourage individuals and business to make the desired expenditures directly. Just as with normal expenditures, these tax losses or "tax expenditures" must be investigated to determine whether society thinks the purposes for which they were designed are public purposes, and to determine whether the tax expenditures actually accomplish their stated objectives, and to see how they influence the structure of demand.

Tax expenditures, however, must meet additional criteria over and above normal expenditure criteria. All special tax provisions interfere with vertical, horizontal, and rank-order equity. As a result of special provisions, individuals with the same incomes are taxed differently. This leads to inversions in rank order and to horizontal inequities. Vertical equity is affected, since the progressive structure of the tax system does not affect all individuals equally. Since the major function of a tax system is to raise revenue equitably for government expenditures and macroeconomic policies, tax expenditures interfere with society's equity goals.

Since tax expenditures produce extra costs, before they can be justified, they must also produce some special benefits over and above what could be produced by direct expenditure programs. At the same time, anything that can be accomplished through special tax provisions can be accomplished through direct expenditures (subsidies). Consequently, there is a general theoretical presumption that taxes should not be used for achieving special social objectives. To make the case for tax expenditures it is necessary to argue that society wants to accomplish some objective, that tax instruments will in fact accomplish that objective, and that tax instruments are clearly superior to any other expenditure instrument for accomplishing that objective. In reality, tax expenditures are usually justified on the grounds that it is possible to get Congress to institute special tax provisions, while it is not possible to get Congress to institute subsidy or expenditure programs for the same purposes.

Our tax expenditures are substantial. In the official estimates of the U.S. Treasury, Federal tax expenditures totaled 48.6 billion dollars in fiscal year 1969 (*see* Table 3-3). In comparison,

TABLE 3-3[1]
Tax Expenditures and Budget Expenditures in Fiscal 1969

	Tax Expenditures (billions)	Budget Expenditures (billions)
National Defense	$0.6	$81.0
International Affairs	0.4	3.9
Agriculture	1.0	5.4
Natural Resources	1.7	1.9
Commerce and Transportation	9.2	8.1
Community Development and Housing	4.7	2.3
Health and Welfare	18.0	48.9
Education and Manpower	0.8	7.2
Veterans	0.6	7.7
Aid to State and Local Governments[2]	4.6	18.3
Capital Gains[3]	7.0	—
Total	$48.6	$184.7

[1]Statement by Joseph W. Barr, Secretary of the Treasury, before the Joint Economic Committee, January 17, 1969.

[2]Tax expenditure estimate is for 1968 while Budget Expenditure is 1968 estimate of grants-in-aid found in National Income Accounts.

[3]This is the midpoint of a range estimate of $4.4 to $8.5 billion.

Federal budget expenditures for the same purposes were $184.7 billion. The largest tax expenditures were for health and welfare, community development and housing, aid to state and local governments, and commerce and transportation. Together these four purposes accounted for $36.5 billion of the total. Practically all of the rest were accounted for by the capital gains provisions. The Treasury calculations did not attribute this tax to any purpose, but it is presumably designed to increase savings and investment, thereby increasing economic growth.

To calculate tax expenditures correctly, it would be necessary to know the ideal tax structure and its impact on economic activities. Given both of these pieces of information it would be possible to estimate revenue yields under the ideal system and the actual system. Deviations between these two yields would be the correct measure of "tax expenditures." Deviations between economic activities in the two systems would be the correct measure of the impact of "tax expenditures."

The Treasury's calculations can be viewed only as a first step toward calculating tax expenditures, since their calculations assume that economic activities would not change if tax expenditures were eliminated.[1] Implicitly this means the Treasury assumed that tax expenditures do not have any impact on economic activity. They consequently do not alter the structure of demand and are merely transfer payments.

Although tax expenditures can be attributed to different purposes, this does not necessarily mean that they in fact accomplish these purposes efficiently or at all. Thus the deductibility of medical expenses reduces federal revenue by approximately $1.5 billion, but does it increase the amount of medical care the American population receives? Special provisions for the oil industry create tax expenditures of $1.6 billion, but do they increase the supply of oil, and is an increase in the supply of oil a social objective? If increasing the supply of oil is a social objective, is there some better method to achieve it? Such questions can be posed to each tax expenditure. Answering them requires a detailed investigation of each area in which tax expenditures are used to promote some objective.[2]

Some areas, however, are easier to analyze. The deductibility of state and local bond interest payments is a case in point. The aim of the provision is to increase the resources of state and local governments; yet a major fraction of the benefits go to bondholders rather than to the intended governments. Consequently, direct subsidies would be a much more efficient method of distributing the intended benefits.

Since most of the tax expenditures are made in the form of deductions or exemptions from taxable income, the existing tax expenditures result in a peculiar set of tax incentives. They are worth more to the high-income taxpayer than to the low-income taxpayer, since a $1 deduction reduces the taxes of a man paying marginal tax rates of 20 percent by 20 cents while reducing the taxes of a man paying marginal tax rates of 70 percent by 70 cents. If a man pays no taxes, he gets no incentives whatsoever. For many of the items listed in the table on tax expenditures, the idea that society wishes to provide more encouragement to the rich than to the poor to make these expenditures is peculiar, to say the least.

Actually, with the exception of a few tax expenditures, such as the medical and drug deductions, most tax expenditures involve a substantial "dead weight loss," since they provide tax deductions for expenditures that would have been carried out in any case. One of the solutions to this problem is to provide deductions only for expenditures in excess of some "normal" level. The normal level for medical and drug deductions is set at 4 percent of income (a level that is too low), but similar normal expenditure levels could be set for other categories.

Given the severe inequities that special tax provisions create in vertical, horizontal, and rank order equity and the possibility of using subsidy programs in place of tax expenditures, there is a general presumption that tax expenditures should be severely reduced, but to the extent that they are effective they influence the structure of demand. They raise it in areas with special provision and lower it in the areas that must pay higher taxes to make up for the tax losses of the special provisions.

Impact on Consumption Expenditure Patterns

Just as the utility-maximizing consumer arranges his savings-consumption decisions to equalize the marginal utility of savings and current consumption, so does he arrange his consumption expenditures to equalize the ratio of the marginal utilities of any two goods to the ratio of their respective prices.[3] When taxes raise the price of a particular good, the individual cuts back on his consumption of that good and increases his consumption of other goods until the relevant ratios are back in equilibrium. In addition to price effects, however, there are income effects. When any particular good is taxed, the consumer's real income is reduced. With a smaller income, he alters his expenditure patterns just as he would if he received a smaller income for some other reasons. As a consequence, both income and substitution effects must be considered to determine the impact of taxes on consumption patterns.

The effects of a general consumption tax have been analyzed in Chapter 2. Basically, under a narrow definition of savings, a one dollar increase in consumption taxes reduced total consumption by 94 cents. Income effects exist for general consumption taxes, but there do not seem to be significant substitution effects toward savings. Another way of expressing this is to say that the income elasticity of demand is one and that the price of elasticity of demand is zero for consumption goods.

To determine the impact of taxes on particular consumption expenditures, income and price elasticities must be estimated for each good in question. The most comprehensive, and best, attempt to measure the relevant elasticities was carried out by Houthakker and Taylor.[4] They found many goods for which the income elasticities of demand were not statistically significantly different from 1 and where the price elasticities of demand were not statistically different from 0 (*see* Table 3-4).

Some of these estimates, especially the price elasticities that cannot be shown to be other than zero, are controversial. Many economists believe that some of these elasticities are not zero, and point to particular commodity studies that have found significant nonzero price elasticities. Although controversial, these estimates are used for several reasons. First, they focus solely on consumption demands. This is important, since many of the commodities purchased by consumers, such as electricity, are also purchased by producers and governments. Production elasticities can be high while consumption elasticities are low.

TABLE 3-4[1]
Income and Expenditure Elasticities of Demand

	Long-Run Income Elasticity	Long-Run Price Elasticity
Alcoholic Beverages	0.62	xx[3]
Food Purchases	0.71	xx
Purchased Meals	x	xx
Tobacco	0.86	−1.89
Shoes and Other Footwear	x[2]	xx
Clothing, Including Luggage	0.51	xx
Space Rental of Owner-occupied Housing	2.45	−1.22
Space Rental of Tenant-Occupied Housing	x	xx
Rental Value of Farm Houses	x	xx
Other Housing	x	xx
Furniture	0.53	xx
Kitchen, and Other Household Appliances	x	xx
Electricity	1.94	−1.89
Gas	x	xx
Telephone, Telegraph, and Wireless	x	xx
Physicians	1.15	xx
Medical Care and Hospitalization Insurance	2.02	−0.92
Interest on Personal Debt	x	xx
New Cars and Net Purchases of Used Cars	1.08	xx
Gasoline and Oil	1.36	xx
Airline Travel	x	xx
Higher Education	x	xx
Foreign Travel by U.S. Residents	3.09	−1.77

[1]The long-run elasticity are taken from the forthcoming revised edition of H. H. Houthakker and Lester D. Taylor, *Consumer Demand in the United States, 1929–1970* (Cambridge, Mass.: Harvard University Press).

[2]Not significantly different from 1.

[3]Not significantly different from 0.

Second, they are both comprehensive and consistent. This means that they cover all areas of consumption and that the individual commodity estimates are consistent with the elasticity of demand for consumption goods in general. Other estimates of demand elasticities exist for specific commodities, but they are not consistent and they tend to mix consumption and production elasticities of demand. Thus the rest of this section will use the Houthakker-Taylor estimates, but the reader should remember their controversial nature.

Although a general consumption tax that reduces real incomes by 1 percent reduces consumption expenditures by the same percentage, the effects differ from commodity to commodity. Purchases of those commodities with income elasticities of demand less than one fall by less than 1 percent and consumption of those commodities with income elasticities of demand greater than one fall by more than 1 percent. Thus food purchases fall by 0.7 percent while electricity purchases fall by 1.9 percent (*see* Table 3-4).

Taxes on commodities with zero price elasticities have exactly the same effects as a general tax on consumption expenditures. They lower real incomes and consumption expenditures, but their impact on the taxed commodity is no greater than the impact that would have occurred with a general sales tax that raised the same revenue.

Although many price elasticities were not statistically significantly different from zero, price elasticities ranged up to -3.8 for radio and television repairs. The major Federal excises are on alcoholic beverages, tobacco, telephones, new cars, gasoline, and airline travel. Since all of these commodities, except tobacco, have zero price elasticities (or at least this hypothesis cannot be rejected) these excise taxes do not alter the pattern of consumption. Since tobacco has a high price elasticity (-1.89), the heavy taxes on tobacco significantly reduce the consumption of tobacco (a 1 percent increase in price reduces sales by 1.89 percent). This excise tax is not equivalent to a general tax on consumption. Most of the effect focuses on tobacco rather than on general consumption expenditures.

The taxes on gasoline and airline travel differ from the other taxes in that they are user charges. As such, they merely price publically provided complementary goods (roads or airports) that are necessary to use the privately provided primary goods (cars or airplanes). If they did not exist and gasoline and air travel had nonzero price elasticities, consumption patterns would be distorted toward too many cars and airplanes since the users would not be paying the full costs of these modes of transportation. Thus, the combination of user taxes and user benefits do not distort consumption patterns. With the zero price elasticities in Table 3-4, however, consumption is not distorted regardless of whether the user taxes are collected or uncollected.

The influence of state and local sales taxes depends upon the price elasticities of the taxed goods (*see* Table 3-4). A general 5 percent sales tax would reduce alcoholic beverages consumption by 3 percent [(5)(0.62)], furniture consumption by 2.5 percent, new-car purchases by 5 percent, and electrical consumption by 10 percent. In terms of revenue collections, the property tax is the largest local tax, but property tax collections amount to only 1.6 percent of market property values.[5] If property investments yield a return of 10 percent per year and the property tax is passed on to the renter (see below), then the property tax would result in a 16 percent increase in the cost of housing.[6] With a − 1.22 price elasticity for owner-occupied housing (*see* Table 3-4), the tax lowers the consumption of housing by 20 percent. The total decline in the consumption of owner-occupied housing would be larger than 20 percent, however, since there is an additional income effect. For a person who spends 25 percent of his income on housing, a 16 percent property tax lowers his real income by 4 percent. Such a reduction leads to another 10 percent reduction [(0.16)(2.45)] in the consumption of owner-occupied housing.

Impact on the Balance of Payments

By influencing prices, incomes, and rates of return on investment, taxes also affect the distribution of economic resources through their impact on exports and imports. This section analyzes the impact of U.S. taxes, but it should be remembered that there is another set of taxes that may be offsetting these impacts or creating impacts of their own. To determine the total impact of taxes on the balance of payments it would be necessary to look at foreign taxes as well as local taxes. Illustrative calculations can be made of the effect of U.S. taxes on our balance of payments, but these calculations assume no response on the part of trading partners. In the long run this is untrue. Since everyone's balance of payments must balance, changes in the American balance of payments will induce changes in foreign policies.

In 1967 import taxes were 5 percent of the value of imports. Assuming that import taxes raised the price of imports 5 percent and that the price elasticity of demand for imports was -0.54 (*see* Table 3-5), tariffs reduced American imports approximately $1.1 billion (1958 dollars) in 1967.[7] Imports, however, are more affected by the income effects of taxes in general than by the price effects of tariffs. The income elasticity of demand for imports is 1.51, but increasing taxes does not affect total incomes as long as the macroeconomic effects of taxes are offset with expenditure policies and monetary policies. Taxes do, however, shift expenditures from the private expenditures to the public expenditures. Since the average public import propensity is only 2 percent while the average private import propensity is 8 percent, shifting resources between sectors can cause a substantial reduction in imports. If such a shift of resources did not take place in the United States, imports would have been $12 billion higher than they were in 1967.

TABLE 3-5[1]
U.S. Pricing and Income Elasticities for Imports and Exports

	Price Elasticity	Income Elasticity
Imports	-0.54	1.51
Exports	-1.51	0.99

[1]H. S. Houthakker and S. P. Magee, "Income and Price Elasticities in World Trade," *Review of Economics and Statistics* (May 1969), p. 113.

Of all the taxes, the corporation income tax is the major American tax affecting U.S. exports. The impact of the corporation income tax, however, depends upon who ultimately pays the tax, a subject of much dispute (*see* Chapter 4). If the tax is shifted backward so that it does not affect prices, it does not affect exports, but it does affect imports; capitalists have lower incomes and import less. If capitalists have average import propensities under the assumption of backward shifting, the corporation income tax reduces imports by $2 billion. If introducing a corporation income tax with an effective rate of 31 percent leads to a 31 percent increase in the price of U.S. exports, American exports were $22 billion lower in 1967 than they would have been without the corporation income tax. (Interpretation of this calculation should be tempered with the knowledge that an elasticity estimate is being used outside of the historical range over which it was estimated.)

The effects of substituting the value-added tax for the corporation income tax—a much discussed alternative—also depends upon the shifting of the corporation income tax. If the corporation income tax were not shifted forward, there would be no favorable effects on our exports. Prices are not higher than they would be with a rebatable value-added tax. If the corporation income tax is shifted forward, exports could increase by as much as $22 billion. If the tax is partially shifted, the results will lie somewhere between these two extremes.

In terms of their impact on the deficit or surplus in our balance of payments, most American taxes are counterbalanced by equivalent foreign taxes. The corporation income tax may be an exception, however. Some countries, principally the Common Market countries, rely on the value-added tax rather than the corporation income tax. Under the rules of GATT a value-added tax can be rebated on exports while the corporation income tax cannot. Thus, exports from these countries bear no taxes while exports from the United States must bear taxes if both the value-added tax and the corporation income tax are shifted forward onto the consumer. As a result, the relative price of American exports rises. If the corporation income tax is not shifted forward, relative prices are not affected, but reductions in the rate of return on exports may lead companies to export less if the tax can be shifted in some domestic areas of the economy.

Shifting to a value-added tax would not lead to a $22 billion increase in U.S. exports even if the corporation income tax were completely reflected in prices. The current system of tariffs, quotas, and exchange rates have been adjusted to current American taxes. If a different U.S. tax structure were going to raise American exports by anything like $22 billion, foreign countries would simply change their tariffs, quotas, and exchange rates to prevent such a change from taking place.

Effects would be small, since policymakers in foreign countries would insure that they were small. Even without changes in international trade policies, some offsetting feedbacks would occur. Variations in our imports and exports would induce changes in foreign incomes and foreign demands for our exports, if they were not offset by foreign macropolicies. Some countries would have higher incomes as a result of an increase in our imports and some countries would have lower incomes as a result of an increase in our exports. Induced exports and imports would be small, however, since income elasticities of demand are generally low (the income elasticity of demand for American exports is 1; *see* Table 3-5). A 1 percent increase in *all* foreign incomes increases our exports by only 1 percent.

While the impact of taxes on imports and exports depends upon the impact of taxes on relative prices and incomes, the impact of taxes on capital flows depends upon the impact of taxes on after-tax rates of return on investment. The interest equalization tax is an example of a tax that was deliberately established to improve the balance of payments by affecting capital flows. Interest earned on accounts held abroad is taxed so that the net interest return is equal to that obtainable in the United States. The impact of the tax depends upon the size of the interest differentials between the United States and the rest of the world, principally Europe. In the early 1950's this tax had an impact on capital flows, since European interest rates were substantially above American levels. As this condition has vanished with rising American interest rates, the impact of the tax has correspondingly fallen.

In this case and in all cases involving capital flows, a sharp distinction must be made between short-run and long-run influences on the balance of payments. Reducing capital outflows improves the balance of payments in the short run while capital is flowing abroad, but makes the balance of payments worse in the long run when earnings or interest would be flowing back into the United States, if the initial investments had been made. Thus, the benefits (or costs) of reducing net capital outflows depends upon the relative value of improving the balance of payments now and in the future.

There are other possible effects from capital outflows. Investment abroad raises incomes abroad and may lead to more exports from the United States. Unless American investment is in those goods that are now imported from the United States, such an increase in our exports will occur. If the investment were in goods that we now export, exports would be likely to fall. In the short run, exports are likely to increase in either case, since American investors abroad will import much of their capital equipment from the United States.

The incidence of the corporation income tax plays a key role in capital flows, since it will reduce the after-tax rate of return to capitalists if it cannot be shifted onto either the consumer or labor. The result will be an added incentive to invest in those countries that do not have a corporation income tax and a net capital outflow in the short run. Thus, the corporation income tax will adversely affect the balance of payments in the short run regardless of whether it is or is not shifted. If it is shifted to the consumer, exports will fall. If it is absorbed by the capitalist, net capital outflows will increase. Only if it is shifted onto labor will it have no impact on the balance of payments.

There are also some special provisions in the tax laws that encourage capital outflows. Investment in underdeveloped countries receives special tax advantages and taxes are not paid on foreign earnings until they are repatriated. Consequently, if the foreign tax rate is less than the American tax rate, some portion of earnings is an interest-free loan of indefinite duration from the government to the company. This provides a tax advantage for foreign investment over domestic investment.

Conclusions

Directly and indirectly taxes create substantial changes in the structure of demand. This raises the incomes earned in some areas and lowers it in others. Except for the direct income transfer programs, however, there is little evidence that tax-induced changes in the structure of demand alter the distributions of income, consumption, or wealth. Individual positions on these distributions change; but the distributions themselves do not change. This result is produced by resource mobility. As demand rises or falls, resources move from the declining sectors to the growing sectors. Thus, tax-induced changes in demand do not seem to affect the distribution of economic resources by income, consumption, or wealth classes.

Notes

1. For a discussion of the strengths and weaknesses of the Treasury calculations see Boris L. Bittker, "Accounting for Federal Tax Subsidies in the National Budget," *National Tax Journal* (June 1969), p. 244, and the ensuing discussion in the *National Tax Journal* (December 1969), Stanley S. Surrey and William F. Hellmuth, "The Tax Expenditure Budget—Response to Professor Bittker," and Boris I. Bittker, "The Tax Expenditure Budget—A Reply to Professors Surrey and Hellmuth."
2. For a general discussion of these "loopholes" see Stephen L. McDonald, *Federal Tax Treatment of Income from Oil and Gas* (Washington, D.C.: The Brookings Institution, 1963); Joseph A. Pechman, *Federal Tax Policy* (Washington, D.C.: The Brookings Institution, 1966); Richard Goode, *The Individual Income Tax* (Washington, D.C.: The Brookings Institution, 1966).
3.
$$\frac{MU_a}{MU_b} = \frac{P_a}{P_b}$$
   where MU_a = marginal utility of good a
   MU_b = marginal utility of good b
   P_a = price of good a
   P_b = price of good b

4. H. S. Houthakker and Lester C. Taylor, *Consumer Demand in the United States, 1929–1970* (Cambridge Mass.: Harvard University Press, 1966), pp. 56–149.
5. Bureau of the Census, *1967 Census of Government—Taxable Property Values*, (Washington, D.C.: Government Printing Office, 1968), pp. 27, 42.
6. Ten percent represents the approximate rate of return on capital investments.
7. These calculations assume that those goods actually taxed have the average relative price elasticity of demand for imports as a whole.

4 The Incidence of Taxes

Tax incidence (the distribution of tax burden) is measured in terms of the changes in the distribution of economic resources with and without taxes. In order to analyze the incidence of taxes, it is necessary to use the microeconomic analysis of the last two chapters to determine who ultimately carries the burden of taxes. What prices are changed, what quantities are altered, and what economic resources rise or fall as a result? These are the essential questions of tax incidence. Since the taxpayer who is legally liable to pay a particular tax can often shift the burden of the tax to someone else by altering the price and/or quantity of whatever he sells, tax incidence is not simply a matter of looking at consumption, incomes, or wealth before and after taxes.[1] It is a matter of looking at these items with and without taxes. Moreover, tax incidence is an area filled with confusion, part of which is created by the problems of making normative judgments about the incidence of taxes (analysis of this problem will be left until Chapter 8) and part by the range of "ceteris parabis" assumptions used in different analyses.

The Ceteris Paribis Assumptions

Government Expenditures. The major "ceteris paribis" assumption revolves around government expenditures. Taxes are used to finance government expenditures that in turn influence the distribution of economic resources. When taxes change, what assumptions are to be made about government expenditures?

There are three standard answers. Government expenditures are assumed to be neutral, they are held constant, or both taxes and expenditures are allowed to vary.

In the context of tax incidence, neutrality means that the government buys exactly the same goods that would have been purchased by the individuals who are forced to pay taxes. With the neutrality assumption, the structure of demand does not change when taxes are imposed. As a result, taxes do not create any expenditure effects that need be analyzed; the same expenditures exist with and without taxes. Although a constant structure of demand simplifies the analysis of tax incidence, the assumption is obviously false. Governments do not buy exactly the same goods that taxpayers would have purchased if they did not have to pay taxes. In fact, the demands are not even similar.

If government expenditures are held constant while taxes are allowed to vary, there are immediate macroeconomic effects. To avoid analyzing the macroeconomic effects of taxes and expenditures, "differential tax incidence" is introduced. Differential tax incidence inquires into the alterations in the distribution of economic resources produced by substituting one tax for another when the two taxes yield the same revenue. Since the two taxes yield the same revenue, it is assumed that the same expenditures can be financed and that macroeconomic effects will not occur. As Chapter 5 will indicate, the latter assumption is incorrect. Different taxes can yield the same revenue, but have different impacts on the economy's aggregate supply and demand for goods and services. Holding government expenditures and government tax revenue constant does not eliminate the possibility of macroeconomic effects that might alter the distribution of economic resources.

It is possible to calculate the changes in different taxes that would have exactly the same macroeconomic effects, but the revenue collections from the different taxes would not necessarily be equal. According to the results in Chapter 5, if personal income taxes were reduced by $1.2 billion, corporate income taxes would need to be increased by $1.6 billion dollars to avoid macroeconomic effects. As a result, differential tax incidence can only be used with the further assumption that monetary policies are being used to offset the unequal macroeconomic effects of equal tax changes. But monetary policies may themselves have an impact on the distribution of economic resources, and taxes with different yields have different direct impacts in the distribution of economic resources. Thus there is no way to avoid the macroeconomic effects of taxes.

The impossibility of abstracting from macroeconomic effects casts doubt on another standard assumption or differential incidence studies. They normally start with the assumption that the economy is held at full employment. There are two objections to the assumption. First, actual economies do not always operate at full employment. Changes in aggregate demand produced by government budgets may be one of the most important methods for altering the distribution of economic resources. Second, the full-employment assumption and the assumptions of differential tax incidence (constant government expenditures and tax revenues) are mutually inconsistent. The economy may start at full employment, government expenditures may be held constant, taxes with equal revenues may be substituted for each other, yet the economy may be forced away from full employment as a result.

Even if it were possible to avoid macroeconomic effects with differential tax incidence, a stiff price is being paid. Differential tax incidence studies may be able to estimate the different distributions of economic resources that would be produced by two sets of taxes with equal revenues, but they are not able to estimate the incidence of any particular tax, since the incidence of the reference tax is unknown. As a consequence, it is only possible to say how the tax under consideration differs from the reference tax.

There is a more fundamental problem with differential tax incidence studies, however. Generally, it is necessary to know the absolute incidence of a tax before it is possible to make a study of differential tax incidence. Knowledge of absolute tax incidence is necessary to calculate the marginal impacts of the two taxes that are being substituted for each other, unless it is possible to find historical instances in which the two taxes under consideration have been substituted for one another and where the distributional impacts of such a change can be determined. In most cases such historical experiments are impossible to find, and even if they are found, isolating the tax effects from all other effects is just as difficult as estimating tax incidence. As a result, differential tax incidence neither produces what is desired nor saves time and effort. Thus the only alternative is to allow both taxes and expenditures to vary.

When both taxes and expenditures are allowed to vary, "budgetary incidence" rather than tax incidence is analyzed. Budgetary incidence suffers from the same macroeconomic problems of differential tax incidence. Lowering both expenditures and taxes by the same amount does not guarantee the elimination of macroeconomic effects. As Chapter 5 will indicate, taxes must fall by more than expenditures to guarantee a constant level of aggregate demand. Thus, macroeconomic incidence cannot be ignored and must be added to budgetary incidence to estimate the total incidence of taxes.

Calculations in this chapter, therefore, will focus on budgetary incidence and calculations in the next chapter will focus on macroeconomic incidence.

Other Assumptions. Incidence studies can also be static or dynamic. Static incidence is the pattern of incidence that would occur in an economy in which the population and productivity are not growing, while dynamic incidence is the pattern of incidence in an economy in which population and productivity are growing. Dynamic incidence is more interesting than static incidence, since actual economies are growing, but a lack of knowledge about dynamic economic systems makes static analysis easier to do. Within dynamic analysis, short-run effects may differ from long-run effects. Many of the items that are fixed in the short run are variable in the long run. The following analysis focuses on long-run comparative statics. Calculations are made on the basis that the economy moves from one position of equilibrium to another position of equilibrium. Since economies are never really in equilibrium, this simplification should be kept in mind when evaluating the results.

Finally, there is the question of market assumptions. Are the neoclassical assumptions of profit maximization, perfectly competitive markets, perfect factor mobility, etc. to be made, or are some of these assumptions to be modified?[7] If the neoclassical assumptions are made, the marginal productivity theory of distribution and the initial ownership of factors of production provide an adequate basis for calculating the distribution of economic resources in the absence of taxes. It is only necessary to determine the marginal return to physical capital and human capital in the absence of government taxes and expenditures.

No one believes that the neoclassical assumptions are met perfectly. The real question is whether the American economy comes close enough to meeting these assumptions to make neoclassical analysis meaningful. The answer is a matter of judgment since there are no conclusive tests either way. In the judgment of the author the economy is competive enough to make neoclassical analysis meaningful, but good arguments can be made to the contrary.

Measures of Tax Incidence

Based on neoclassical investment theory, individuals invest in capital, either human or physical, until the marginal private rate of return is equal to the rate of time preference. When a tax is imposed on wealth (directly or indirectly) investors will reduce investment until the pretax rate is high enough to yield a posttax rate of return that is equal to the rate of time preference. The posttax rate of return will not change unless the investor's rate of time preference changes.

Theoretically, taxes can either increase or decrease an investor's rate of time preference. Individual rates of time preference are normally assumed to be a function of an individual's income (the wealthier he is the lower his rate of time preference), but there are both income and substitution effects to be considered. If taxes lower an investor's present and future income the individual may lower his rate of time preference (increase his savings) to restore future consumption levels or he may raise his rate of time preference (lower his savings) to restore current consumption. Which of these two will take place depends on the rate of substitution between current and future income and the size of the cut in income due to taxes. Assuming that the individual's only motivation for savings is future consumption, that he has a constant decreasing marginal utility of income schedule over time, and that he will be wealthier in the future than he is in the present, the imposition of a proportional or progressive income tax will cause the individual to raise his rate of time preference to restore his current consumption standards. Therefore, imposition of such an income tax system would lead to an observed increase in the rate of return on investment both before and after taxes. The individual's higher rate of time preference would lead him to demand a higher after-tax rate of return on investment than before. With a regressive tax structure the individual effects could go either way. The results would depend on the regressiveness of the tax structure and the rate at which the marginal utility of income falls.

In a world in which the individual saves for economic power as well as future consumption, additional possibilities appear. Taxes reduce current economic power (wealth) as well as consumption. Consequently, the individual may increase his savings to increase his current economic power. Thus the rate of time preference might fall rather than rise, leading to a decrease in the observed after-tax rate of return on investment.

Tax burdens or incidence are often measured in terms of changes in the after-tax rate of return on capital, but they should not be. Changes in the posttax rate of return provides evidence about the impact of taxes on the rate of time preference, but they do not provide evidence about tax burdens. Viewed from this perspective the Krzyaniak-Musgrave evidence that the imposition of the corporation income tax caused a slight increase in the after-tax rate of return on capital makes complete sense.[2] Such evidence indicates that the corporation income tax caused investor's rate of time preference to rise. It does not indicate that the tax was shifted by more than 100 percent.

Income shares are an alternative measure of tax burdens, but income shares ignore any reduction in output (excess burden) caused by the imposition of taxes. As a result they do not really provide an adequate measure of tax impacts. Tax burdens should be measured in terms of their changes in an individual's wealth and consumption. Both are necessary because an investor who cuts back on his investment to raise his after-tax rate of return to the level required by his rate of time preference will reduce his total wealth but increase his consumption. Consumption gains (or losses) will be algebraically equal to the changes in savings with and without taxes. Changes in wealth, however, will depend upon the impact on the after-tax rate of return as well as changes in the quantity of resources since the resources will be capitalized at different rates.

If the rate of time preference does not change and small changes in the capital stock cause large changes in the marginal product of capital (i.e., a low elasticity of output with respect to capital) then taxes on wealth (human or physical) or on income from wealth will have little impact on an individual's total wealth or consumption (only small changes in savings are necessary). If time preferences do change or if elasticities are large, changes in investment and savings will be substantial. In a dynamic economy, the ultimate incidence also depends upon technical progress. Technical progress may cause the marginal productivity of capital to rise. If it does, the faster the technical progress, the less each individual must cut back his savings and investment to keep the posttax rate of return equal to the rate of time preference.

Laborers make a set of calculations that are similar to those of capitalists when they decide to furnish labor. The individual invests in his own human capital until the after-tax rate of return on human capital equals his rate of time preference, but the rate of return in human capital is partially determined by the marginal disutility of work. The individual will use his human capital (work) until the wage rate is brought into equilibrium with the marginal disutility of work. The imposition of a tax on labor thus affects the amount of labor supplied through its direct effect on the after-tax wage rate, but it also may influence the point at which the marginal utility of income and leisure are equal. With a lower income, the normal individual will have a higher marginal utility of income and thus must increase his work effort to bring the utilities of leisure and income into balance. Such income and substitution effects could lead the individual to work more or less as a result of a tax, just as they could lead capitalists to invest more or less as a result of a tax. But for either capitalists or laborers, it is necessary to look at both consumption and wealth to determine the distributional impact of taxes.

Taxes on Capital and Labor

Corporation Income Taxes, Personal Income Taxes, and Social Insurance Taxes. As shown in Chapter 2, aggregate production functions make it possible to translate tax-induced changes in the supplies of capital and labor into changes in output.[3] In addition, however, they provide a method for estimating the marginal products of capital and labor for different stocks of capital and labor.[4] As a result, it is possible to estimate the elasticities of the marginal product schedules (the rate at which the marginal product falls as its supply increases). When combined with knowledge about changes in the rate of time preference or in the marginal disutility of work. These marginal product elasticities can be used to determine how much the stocks of labor and capital would need to change to bring workers and investors back into equilibrium after the imposition of taxes.

For example, if the rate of time preference of capitalists does not change with the imposition of taxes, capitalists' required rates of return on capital investment do not change with the imposition of taxes. Thus the imposition of a 50 percent corporate income tax requires a reduction in the stock of capital to bring the after-tax rate of return back into equilibrium with the capitalist's required rate of return. If the elasticity of output with respect to capital is 0.3, a 1 percent increase in the capital stock lowers the marginal productivity of capital by 0.7 percent in a simple Cobb Douglas Production function. Thus a 3.5 percent [(50)(0.7)] increase in the capital stock would be necessary to bring the rate of return back to the rate of time preference after the elimination of a 50 percent income tax.

To some extent marginal product elasticities are substitutes for the participation functions, hours of work functions, and investment functions used in Chapter 2, and to some extent they are complimentary. In general the elasticity approach yields estimates of long-run impacts while the labor and capital supply functions yield estimates of short-run impacts.

The major problem in the elasticities approach is finding the correct aggregate production function. The problem is çreated by the fact that econometric production functions produce different elasticities than would be deduced from looking at the distribution of output between capital and labor. Since the two estimates should be identical, but are not (econometrically estimated elasticities of output with respect to capital are lower than functional share estimates), there is a problem of picking the right estimate. For the purposes of this book, however, the two types of estimates are not so divergent that they must be resolved. Thus the estimates in Chapter 2 used an econometrically fitted production function while the estimates in this section will use elasticities derived from functional shares.

Analysis of the distribution of output in the American economy indicates that the elasticity of output with respect to capital is 0.3 and that the elasticity of output with respect to labor is 0.7.[5] Economies or diseconomies of scale do not seem to play an important role at the level of our entire economy, but a problem arises as to the correct form of the aggregate production function. Most evidence suggests an elasticity of substitution between capital and labor in the neighborhood of 0.6.[6] Consequently, a Constant Elasticity of Substitution (CES) production function is used in this analysis rather than the more common Cobb-Douglas form of the function. Technical progress is also assumed to be embodied in new capital investment. Some evidence indicates that this occurs at the rate of 4.0 percent per year.[7]

In 1965 the average effective tax rate on capital earnings was 13.5 percent.[8] Given that the rate of time preference has not significantly changed with the imposition of the corporation income tax (the Musgrave-Krzyaniak results), the change in the capital stock that would be necessary to hold the after-tax marginal product of capital at 1965 levels, if taxes on capital were eliminated, is easily calculated. It would have had to expand by 21 percent.[9] Such an increase would, of course, have repercussions on output and the before-tax marginal product of labor; output would have increased by 6 percent and the marginal product of labor would have risen by 10 percent. Labor's marginal product would rise since it would be working with more capital.

On the labor side, assume a constant marginal utility of income is equivalent to assuming a constant rate of time preference on the capital side. But there is no supporting evidence for this assumption in the labor side. Labor supply function (*see* Chapter 2) indicated that the marginal income fell as income rose. Income effect dominated substitution effect. Every 1 percent increase in after-tax incomes decreased labor effort by 0.07 percent. Using these results eliminating taxes on labor (personal income taxes and social insurance taxes) would reduce the supply of labor by 0.9 percent.[10] Such a reduction would have cut the marginal product of capital by 1 percent and output by 0.6 percent.

If both capital and labor taxes had been eliminated at the same time, there would be further ramifications. Increasing the capital stock would raise labor's marginal product and lead to less labor being supplied to the market. Reductions in the supply of labor would lower the marginal product of capital and lead to reductions in the stock of capital. If all income taxes and social insurance taxes had been eliminated the capital stock would have expanded by 19.6 percent, and the labor stock would have contracted by 1.6 percent after all ramifications have been taken into account.

In 1965 the gross incomes of capital and labor were $188 billion, and $419 billion respectively. Their after-tax incomes were $119 billion and $362 billion. Without taxes, their incomes would have been $224 billion and $412 billion. Taxes on capital earnings of $69 billion reduced the incomes of capitalists by $106 billion with an excess burden of $36 billion ($224 − $188). On the labor side, tax collections of $57 billion reduced labor's income by $50 billion. Labor's reduction in after-tax incomes is not as large as tax collections because labor worked more as a result of the taxes.

At the same time, individuals had to reduce their leisure time to increase their working time by 1.6 percent. Since individuals had less leisure, individual utility levels will be lower than a simple $50 billion reduction in incomes would indicate, but the $7 billion that individuals earned in this way is presumably more valuable to *them* than the lost leisure.

Capitalists' after-tax incomes would have been $106 billion higher without taxes, but just as laborers have to work harder to earn their higher incomes, capitalists have to save more to earn their higher incomes. In fact, they would have to save $149 billion more and consume $149 billion less in order to reap their increased incomes. Thus to measure the net gains in capitalists' economic welfare it would be necessary to subtract the value of $149 billion in consumption expenditures from the benefits of a gross increase in annual capital incomes streams of $37 billion and an after-tax net increase of $106 billion.

If excess burdens are viewed in terms of income alone, there is a positive excess burden of $37 billion in the capital sector and a negative excess burden of $7 billion in the labor sector.[12] The net burden in terms of output is thus $30 billion. If the three taxes under consideration had been eliminated, the output of the economy would be $30 billion higher than it actually was. Thus viewing incidence in terms of income alone, a $1 increase in labor taxes reduces labor's income by $0.88 and a $1 increase in capital taxes reduces capitalists' incomes by $1.53.

Consumption Taxes. In addition to their impacts on saving-consumption decisions, consumption taxes have an impact on real take-home incomes and wage rates. They represent a reduction in real after-tax marginal products for both capital and labor. If no one suffers from money illusion, consumption taxes would cause the same changes as those created by income taxes. The capitalist would invest until his real after-tax rate of return were equal to his rate of time preference, and the laborer would work until the real after-tax marginal utility of income equaled the marginal disutility of work. With money illusion, consumption taxes do not affect supplies of capital and labor and are simply a burden on individuals in proportion to their consumption expenditures. Money illusion may exist, but it is in the spirit of this section to assume that the consumer is also a neoclassical man who makes his decisions in real terms rather than in monetary terms. He does not suffer from money illusion.

In 1965 consumption taxes amounted to 8.8 percent of personal outlays ($39.3 billion), but the tax was higher on labor than on capital since capitalists saved 13 percent of their personal income, while laborers saved only 4.7 percent.[13] Consequently, when consumption taxes are added to income taxes and social insurance taxes, the effective tax rate for capitalists rises to 39.4 percent and for laborers to 20.8 percent. If income taxes, social insurance taxes, and consumption taxes were eliminated, the capital stock would need to increase by 21 percent and the labor stock would need to fall by 2.5 percent to restore equilibrium. Eliminating consumption taxes would thus result in an additional increase in capitalist's real incomes of $26.6 billion. (In money terms labor's income would fall by $3.8 billion.) Consumption taxes thus produce a positive excess burden of $2.8 billion from their impact on capitalists and a negative excess burden of $3.8 billion from their impact on labor. The net excess burden is thus $1.0 billion. Thus consumption taxes create tax burdens in proportion to the individual's consumption expenditures, but they also create small excess burdens that must be distributed.[14]

Property Taxes. Theoretically the incidence of the property tax could be estimated with the same technique, but the data do not exist to estimate formal production functions for what might be called the "space rental industry." The property tax is peculiar, however, in that it can be divided into a property tax on land and a property tax on buildings. Since there is a fixed supply of land, the supply elasticity of land is zero. As a result, taxes cannot influence the supply of land, or its gross marginal product. Consequently, that part of the property tax assessed on land cannot be shifted. It must reside as a burden on the land owner. On the other hand, the long-run supply elasticity of buildings is infinite. Hence that part of the tax that is assessed on buildings must reside as a burden on the renter or user.

Excess burdens may be created, however, if the higher user

costs for buildings lead to lower usage and less construction.
The Houthakker-Taylor study of price and income elasticities
of demand found an elasticity of -1.2 for the space rental value
of owner-occupied housing, but did not find price elasticities
significantly different from zero for tenant-occupied housing,
farm housing, or other housing (hotels, cabins, schools, institutions, etc.).[15] (Their study did not include commercial or industrial buildings.) If these elasticities are correct, a property
tax of 1.6 percent (the average U.S. rate on market values) would
lead in the long run to a 1.6 percent increase in the space rental
price of owner-occupied housing and a 1.9 percent reduction
$((1.6)(-1.2))$ in the consumption of owner-occupied housing.
Thus the excess burden (reduction in output) of the tax would
be greater than the size of the property tax itself. As a result,
building owners would save less and their property incomes
would fall by 1.9 percent. The real income of users would fall
because of the 1.6 percent increase in the price of housing. The
net reductions in real incomes of users would depend upon
what fraction housing payments were in their total incomes.
Since the average American family spends 13 percent of its
disposable personal income on shelter, the average family's real
income would be reduced by 0.2 percent $((1.6)(0.18))$.[16] Since the
user and the owner are the same person in owner-occupied
housing, reduction in incomes would be 2.1 percent. But part of
this loss, however, could be recouped since the resources that
would have been invested in housing could be invested in
something else. If the rate of return on housing investments and
other investments are identical, the net reduction in income
would be 0.2 percent.

Property taxes are peculiar, however, in that they are to some
extent voluntary taxes. Although property taxes are not voluntary for many individuals that must live in particular communities, they are voluntary in large metropolitan areas where
individuals can choose between suburban areas that are roughly
equivalent except for property taxes and public services. The
individual chooses to live in a particular community with a
known set of property taxes but also with a known set of public
expenditures. Property taxes are a cost and public services are

a benefit. As long as the individual thinks the benefits of public services exceed the costs of property taxes, he will choose to live in the area. If there are enough people who want public services, providing public services and levying the necessary property taxes may raise market values rather than lower them. In a recent study for Northern New Jersey, Oates found that the negative effects of property taxes and the positive effects of public services seem to have equal but offsetting influences, leaving property values unaffected.[17] Thus, when property taxes are under consideration, budgetary incidence studies, such as those carried out in the next section, are almost a necessity.

At the moment the data necessary to estimate the precise incidence of the property tax are unavailable. It would be necessary to know the relative values of land and buildings in property tax assessments, the percentage of the population that can actually choose where they want to live based upon a menu of property taxes and public services, and the elasticity of demand for commercial and industrial buildings. Not having all of this information, it is necessary to use an assumption based upon judgment rather than hard evidence. In the following incidence calculations the property tax will be assumed to rest 50 percent on property owners and 50 percent on users. If the owner and user are identical, he obviously pays 100 percent of the tax.

Distributions of Economic Resources

Income. Using the results of the previous section, the existing distributions of income and consumption and the cross-distribution of income and wealth, it is possible to construct the budgetary incidence of taxes and expenditures.[18] These calculations are based on the assumption that macroeconomic conditions are not affected, but this assumption will be relaxed in the next chapter. Since the calculations indicate the changes that are produced in individual incomes with the elimination of taxes and expenditures, they must include the excess burdens of taxes as well as the direct effects. Since the excess burdens of capitalists are positive, their incomes would go up by more than the magnitude of the tax reduction. Conversely, labor finds that its income does not go up by the magnitude of the tax reduction since it works less and takes more leisure (it has a negative excess burden).

The analysis indicates that the tax system has a basically proportional effect on incomes until incomes of $10,000 per year are reached (*see* Table 4-1).[19] Above this level the tax system becomes progressive, not so much because of the taxes that are actually collected, but because of the excess burdens that are imposed on capitalists. Personal taxes are generally progressive throughout the income distribution, while corporate taxes are basically proportional until high incomes are reached. Social insurance taxes and consumption taxes are both regressive, since they apply only to labor income and to consumption expenditures. Property taxes have a U-shaped pattern. Since half of their incidence is assumed to be on the consumer, they are high at low-income levels, where consumption is relatively high, but they are also high at high-income levels because their incidence is assumed to be half on property owners.

Expenditure benefits generally fall as income rises, but the results for general benefits depend upon the assumption that half of the benefits of general expenditures can be distributed on the basis of population and half of the benefits can be distributed on the basis of income. Nongeneral benefits, distributed on the basis of the actual beneficiary, prove to be even more progressively distributed than general benefits.

When taxes and expenditures are combined, budgets prove to be progressively distributed. Net benefits rise as incomes rise. In aggregate, there is a net income transfer of from $25 billion to $30 billion per year from those with incomes over $7,500 to those with incomes of less than $7,500. The changes caused by taxes and expenditures can be seen by looking at the impacts on an individual who would have an income of $1,000 in a world without taxes and an individual who would have an income of $20,000 in a world without taxes. With taxes, the before-tax incomes of these individuals is currently $992 and $17,980 respectively, after taxes their take-home incomes are $749 and $8,700.[20] For these two men the benefits of public expenditures

TABLE 4-1[1]

Budgetary Incidence as a Percentage of Total Income for All Families by Income Class, 1965

	Under $2,000	$2,000 to 2,999	$3,000 to 3,999	$4,000 to 4,999	$5,000 to 5,999	$6,000 to 7,499	$7,500 to 9,999	$10,000 to 14,999	$15,000 and over	Total
Taxes										
Personal	2.9	3.8	5.2	6.9	7.2	7.9	9.1	10.7	28.2	9.6
Corporate	1.2	2.1	4.3	1.7	2.3	1.7	2.0	5.4	15.5	3.8
Social Insurance	4.1	4.2	4.5	4.8	4.6	4.4	4.2	3.9	2.1	4.2
Consumption	9.8	8.5	8.6	7.9	7.5	7.0	6.4	5.9	4.4	6.9
Property	7.1	5.3	4.5	3.7	3.4	3.1	3.1	3.4	6.3	3.8
Total Taxes	25.1	23.9	27.1	25.0	25.0	24.1	24.8	29.3	56.5	28.3
Expenditures										
General Benefit	46.2	26.7	21.2	17.9	16.0	14.3	12.8	11.3	9.3	15.6
Defense and International	26.2	15.1	12.0	10.1	9.0	8.1	7.2	6.4	5.3	8.8
Other	20.0	11.6	9.2	7.8	7.0	6.2	5.6	4.9	4.0	6.9
Nongeneral Benefits	62.8	38.3	24.8	15.8	13.4	11.1	9.3	8.7	6.9	14.3
Total Expenditures	109.0	65.0	46.0	33.7	29.5	25.4	22.1	20.0	16.3	29.9
Total	83.9	41.1	18.9	8.7	4.5	1.3	-2.7	-9.3	-40.2	1.6

[1]Calculated by modifying the results of *Tax Burdens and Benefits of Government Expenditures By Income Class, 1961 and 1965* (New York: Tax Foundation, Inc., 1961, 1967).

are $1,090 and $3,260 respectively. As a proportion of his income the rich man receives less by way of public expenditures, but in absolute terms he receives three times as much as the poor man. Consequently, their real incomes are $1,839 and $11,960.

Consumption. The impact on the distribution of consumption expenditures depends upon whether the period being examined is the period in which capitalists are cutting their consumption expenditures to build up the stock of capital or the period after the capital stock has reached desired levels. In the short run the former is relevant, and in the long run the latter is relevant. Table 4-2 presents information on the distribution of private consumption expenditures in 1960–61, the distribution of private plus public consumption expenditures, and the long-run distribution of private consumption expenditures in a world without taxes and expenditures. The distribution of public plus private consumption expenditures is less disperse than the distribution of private consumption expenditures, but both of these are less

TABLE 4-2[1]
Impact of Taxes and Expenditures on Consumption

Distribution (%)	Consumption Classes		
	Private Consumption ($)	Public Plus Private Consumption ($)	Private Consumption Without Taxes and Expenditures ($)
2.7	0–1,000	0–1,872	0–1,251
9.7	1,000–1,999	1,872–3,390	1,252–2,489
11.1	2,000–2,999	3,391–4,331	2,490–3,764
11.9	3,000–3,999	4,332–5,275	3,765–5,041
13.0	4,000–4,999	5,276–6,264	5,042–6,249
28.7	5,000–7,499	6,265–8,924	6,250–9,336
13.7	7,500–9,999	8,925–11,638	9,337–12,704
7.1	10,000–14,999	11,639–17,174	12,705–21,434
2.1	15,000 and up	17,175 and up	21,435 and up

[1]Calculated by modifying the initial distribution of consumption expenditures found in Lenore A. Epstein, "Measuring the Size of the Low Income Population," *Six Papers on the Size Distribution of Wealth and Income*, Lee Soltow, ed. (New York: National Bureau of Economic Research, 1969), p. 190. All public expenditures are treated as if they are public consumption expenditures.

disperse than the distribution of private consumption expenditures in a world without taxes and expenditures. In 1960–61, 28.7 percent of the population had private consumption expenditures between $5,000 and $7,499. The same group of individuals had private plus public consumption expenditures of between $6,265 and $8,924. Without taxes and expenditures this group of individuals would have private consumption expenditures of between $6,250 and $9,336. In terms of total consumption expenditures (public plus private), the bottom 48 percent of the population has more consumption expenditures with taxes and expenditures while the top 52 percent of the population would have more consumption expenditures in a world without taxes and expenditures. Thus taxes and expenditures provide a substantial equalization of consumption. On the other hand, they still leave large absolute differences between the consumption standards of the top 10 percent of the population and the bottom 10 percent of the population. In terms of private consumption, the top 2.1 percent of the population enjoy 5.7 percent of all private consumption expenditures, but in terms of public plus private consumption expenditures they enjoy only 5.1 percent. If taxes and expenditures had been eliminated, however, they would enjoy 7.0 percent of all consumption expenditures.

Given fixed marginal propensities to consume, changes are not hard to bring about in the distribution of consumption expenditures. Taxes are simply levied on income in such a way that the desired distribution of consumption expenditures is produced. If wealth is simply capitalized income, then income taxes can be used to determine consumption expenditures regardless of whether consumption is affected by income, wealth, or both.

Leisure. Without taxes and expenditures the distribution of leisure would be more equal. Adult men, the group working the most hours, would work less because of the income effects, while women and teen-agers, the group working the shortest hours, would work more because of the substitution effect. The result would be a 2.5 percent increase in the average hours of leisure with substantial equalization around the average number of hours worked.

Wealth. Proceeding on the same set of assumptions used to allocate taxes across the income distribution, it is possible to allocate taxes across the distribution of wealth. Consumption taxes have no impact on the distribution of wealth under these assumptions, but the excess burden of taxes on capital is again important and included in the analysis. Some taxes, such as the property tax, are direct taxes on wealth, but most taxes are levied on incomes and only indirectly affect the net worth of an individual. These indirect effects occur through a process of capitalizing tax payments into net worth. Taxes reduce net income flows and thus reduce the capitalized private present value of any asset (future stream of earnings). Many of the taxes such as property taxes, corporation income taxes, and automobile taxes are levied at flat rates, which do not depend upon the individual's income or upon his total wealth. These taxes have the same proportional effect on the wealth of the rich and the poor. Other taxes, such as the personal income tax, are progressive. When these taxes are capitalized, they will have larger impact on the wealth of the rich than of the poor since the wealthy pay higher tax rates than the poor. Thus a given stream of future income is worth more to a poor man with low income tax rates than to a wealthy man with high income tax rates. Consequently, removing progressive income taxes serves to cause a greater proportional increase in the net worth of the wealthy than in the net worth of the poor (*see* Appendix).

Given the incomplete coverage of wealth taxes many types of wealth are not taxed. These would include life insurance policies, annuities, retirement plans, trusts, and unrealized capital gains on all types of wealth. Different types of wealth are taxed at different rates. Corporate wealth must pay the corporation income tax, and property wealth must pay the property tax. Thus, the effective tax rate on net worth depends not only on the total amount of net worth but also upon its composition.

Effective tax rates on wealth range from 4.5 percent for those with negative net worths to 31.1 percent for those with net worths between $20,000 and $49,999; but most of the progression comes before net worths of only $5,000 (*see* Table 4-3). For the very wealthy, tax rates start to fall just as they do in the income tax. Thus, the group with over $500,000 in net worth has an effective tax rate of only 27.2 percent.

TABLE 4-3[1]
Net Worth with and Without Taxes

Size of Net Worth ($)	Total Net Worth			Total Net Worth Without Taxes and Assuming No Excess Burden ($)	Tax Rate (%)
	With Taxes ($)	Without Taxes ($)	Tax Rate (%)		
Negative	−538	−514	4.5	−519	3.7
0–999	302	340	11.2	339	10.9
1,000–4,999	2,809	3,372	16.7	3,341	15.9
5,000–9,999	7,305	9,146	20.1	9,041	19.2
10,000–24,999	16,281	20,760	21.6	20,352	20.0
25,000–49,999	35,309	44,874	21.3	43,325	18.5
50,000–99,999	67,042	87,942	23.8	81,035	17.3
100,000–199,999	129,958	181,906	28.6	156,319	16.9
200,000–499,999	293,655	426,483	31.1	352,933	16.8
500,000 and over	1,176,281	1,615,250	27.2	1,358,142	13.4
Total	22,588	30,118	25.0	27,216	17.0

Cumulative Distribution of Wealth

Households (%)	With Taxes (%)	Without Taxes (%)	Without Taxes and No Excess Burden (%)
8.1	−0.2	−0.1	−0.2
25.4	0.0	0.1	0.0
42.7	2.1	2.0	2.1
56.9	6.6	6.2	6.7
81.3	23.8	22.6	24.5
92.5	40.9	38.9	41.9
97.6	55.6	53.4	56.7
98.6	61.3	59.4	62.4
99.5	74.2	73.5	75.3
100.0	100.0	100.0	100.0

[1]Calculations based on average portfolios for individuals in different net worth classes as found in Board of Governors of Federal Reserve System, "Survey of Financial Characteristics," *Federal Reserve Bulletin* (March, 1964), p. 289.

Above net worths of $24,999, all of the increase in effective tax rates is produced by the excess burden of the taxes rather than by the tax collections themselves. Assuming no excess burdens, tax rates rise from 3.7 percent for those with negative net worths to 20.0 percent for those with net worths from $10,000 to $24,999. Above $24,999, effective tax rates gradually fall to 13.4 percent for those with more than $500,000 in net worth. Thus, in the short run, before capitalists have had a chance to alter the capital stock (and their saving-consumption decisions), wealth taxes are very progressive over the low ranges of net worth, and then become quite regressive over the upper ranges of net worth.

Since most of the population has low net worths (81 percent of the population has a net worth of less than $24,999), taxes do not have much impact on the distributions of wealth with or without the assumption of excess burden (*see* Table 4-3). The lower 81.3 percent of the population currently has 23.8 percent of total wealth, but it would have only 22.6 percent of the wealth in a world without taxes and without excess burdens. In contrast, the top 0.5 percent of the population currently has 15.8 percent of total wealth. Without taxes it would have 16.5 percent of total wealth, and without taxes and excess burden it would have 14.7 percent of total wealth. The concentration of wealth among the upper 19 percent of the nation's households means that the distribution of wealth can only be significantly affected with heavy taxes on these households. Reducing wealth taxes for the rest of the population would have almost no impact on the distribution of wealth. Lowering wealth taxes for a man with no wealth does not affect his wealth.

Wealth taxes, however, are the place where society is forced to balance the goals of achieving its desired distribution of wealth and its desired growth targets. The excess burden of a tax which would achieve society's desired distribution of wealth would have a substantial impact on the level of output.

Human Capital. Capitalizing at a 10 percent rate it is possible to transform the distribution of earned income (wages and salaries) into a distribution of human capital (*see* Table 4-4).

TABLE 4-4[1]
Distribution of Human Capital

Percent of Population	After Taxes	Without Taxes and No Excess Burden	Without Taxes
6.0	$0–4,990	$0–4,990	$0–4,990
4.4	4,991–9,840	4,991–9,990	4,991–9,972
4.5	9,841–14,210	9,991–14,990	9,973–14,896
3.1	14,211–18,690	14,991–19,990	14,897–19,833
4.0	18,691–23,170	19,991–24,990	19,834–24,730
3.6	23,171–27,650	24,991–29,990	24,731–29,707
4.5	27,651–32,230	29,991–34,990	29,708–34,657
4.6	36,231–36,750	34,991–39,990	34,658–39,598
5.1	36,751–41,260	39,991–44,990	39,599–44,539
5.1	41,261–45,790	44,991–49,990	44,540–49,482
12.1	45,791–54,830	49,991–59,990	49,483–59,366
10.6	54,831–63,550	59,991–69,990	59,367–69,211
8.0	63,551–72,070	69,991–79,990	69,212–79,032
10.8	72,071–88,790	79,991–99,990	79,033–98,635
10.5	88,791–130,190	99,991–149,990	98,636–147,594
2.5	130,191–204,990	149,991–249,990	147,595–244,545
0.4	204,991 and over	249,991 and over	244,546 and over

[1]Based on labor earnings found in Census Bureau, *Current Population Reports, Consumer Income, 1962*, Series P-60, no. 41 (Washington, D.C.: Government Printing Office, 1962), p. 50.

Since the personal income tax is progressive, the personal income tax serves to equalize the distribution of human capital. After taxes, the bottom 6.0 percent of the population had human capitals of less than $4,990, while the top 0.4 percent of the population had human capitals of more than $204,991. Without personal taxes, the respective human capitals are $4,990 and $244,568, and without personal taxes and with no excess burden (labor has a negative excess burden—i.e., taxes make it work more) the respective human capitals are $4,990 and $249,991. Thus, part of the equalizing impact of progressive personal income taxes was offset by changes in work effort.

Conclusions

The income distributions calculated in this chapter indicate the tax system is more progressive than most other incidence studies have indicated, but most of the progressivity of the tax system depends upon the excess burdens that it creates. This is disturbing because it means that the present tax system can only create progressivity by reducing output. The division of the economic pie is made more equal by making everyone's slice smaller. Whether this creates an improvement in economic welfare will be left to Chapter 8, but simple economic efficiency would call for the establishment of a tax structure that could create progressivity without large excess burdens. This might be accomplished by replacing income taxes with a combination of consumption and wealth taxes. If the relative rates were set correctly, these two taxes could raise the necessary revenue without creating large reductions in the supply of capital. Consumption taxes would be set to increase savings and wealth taxes would be used to obtain society's desired distribution of economic resources.

At the same time the reader should be aware that the large excess burdens are produced by the technique of using marginal product elasticities derived from production functions and functional shares. Econometric investment functions typically yield much smaller excess burdens (*see* Chapter 2). I have argued that investment functions yield short-run as opposed to long-run effects, but this may not be true. If it is not true, the excess burdens should be scaled downward to be compatible with the earlier results.

Both the existing distribution of wealth and the effective taxes rates upon wealth raise serious questions about the adequacy of wealth taxation and the adequacy of using income taxes to control the distribution of wealth. It is highly unlikely that society wants 2.4 percent of the population to control 44 percent of all private assets or that it wants a regressive structure of wealth taxes.

Thus both of the fundamental problems discovered in this chapter point to a serious investigation of wealth taxation, a subject that will be discussed in Chapter 7.

Notes

1. For a general summary of incidence theory see Peter Mieszkowski, "Tax Incidence Theory: The Effects of Taxes on the Distribution of Income," *Journal of Economic Literature* (December, 1969).
2. M. Krzyaniak and R. A. Musgrave, *The Shifting of the Corporation Income Tax* (Baltimore, Md.: The John Hopkins Press, 1963). For other articles in connection with the Krzyaniak and Musgrave results see J. C. Cragg, A. C. Harberger, and P. Mieszkowski, "Empirical Evidence of the Incidence of the Corporation Income Tax," *Journal of Political Economy* (December 1967); R. J. Gordon, "The Incidence of the Corporation Income Tax in U.S. Manufacturing," *American Economic Review* (September 1967); M. Krzyaniak, ed., *Effects of Corporation Tax*, Detroit, Mich.: Wayne State University Press, 1966.
3. For the first attempt to implement this approach see Challis A. Hall, Jr., *Direct Shifting and the Taxation of Corporate Profits in Manufacturing 1919–1959* (M.I.T.: Ph.D. Thesis in Economics).
4. *See* Footnotes 8 and 9, below.
5. These are gross shares of private GNP as found in the *Survey of Current Business* (July 1967) (Washington, D.C.: Government Printing Office), p. 15.
6. Ronald G. Bodkin and Lawrence R. Klien, "Nonlinear Estimation of Aggregate Production Functions," *The Review of Economics and Statistics* (February 1967), p. 39.
7. Lester C. Thurow and L. D. Taylor, "The Interaction Between the Actual and Potential Rates of Growth," *The Review of Economics and Statistics* (November 1966), p. 356.
8. Calculated from *Survey of Current Business* (July 1967), p. 15.
9. Calculate according to the following equations:
   CES Production Function

   $$\gamma(t) = Ae^{\alpha t}[(1-\lambda)K_x(t)^{-p} + (\lambda)L_z(t)^{-p}]^{-\alpha/p}$$

   The Marginal Product of Capital

   $$\frac{Y(t)}{I(t)} = Ae^{\alpha t}(\gamma)\left[(1-\lambda)K_x(t)^{-p} + \lambda L_z(t)^{-p}\right]^{(-\gamma/p-1)} + (1-\lambda)K_x(t)^{(-p-1)}(1+x)^t.$$

10. The Marginal Product of Labor

    $$\frac{Y(t)}{L(t)} = Ae^{\alpha t}(\gamma)\left[(1-\lambda)K_x(t)^{-p} + \lambda L_z(t)^{-p}\right]^{(-\gamma/p-1)} + (\lambda)[(1+z)^t]^{-p}L(t)^{(-p-1)}$$

    where
    $\sigma = 1/1 + p =$ elasticity of substitution of capital for labor
    $=$ output
    $t =$ time
    $K_x =$ utilized capital stock measured in efficiency units
    $$K_x(t) = \left\{\sum_{v=-\infty}^{t}(1+x)^v B(t-v)I(v)\right\}(R)$$
    $I(v) =$ investment in year v
    $R =$ rate of utilization
    $B(t-v) =$ amount of capital investment from year v surviving in year t
    $x =$ rate of embodiment in capital
    $L_z =$ utilized labor manhours measured in efficiency units
    $L_x = L(1+z)^t$

11. Office of Business Economics, *Survey of Current Business* (July 1967), p. 15.

12. The negative excess burden is only in terms of income. There is a positive excess burden in terms of having less leisure.

13. Based on the distributions of net worth found in *Federal Reserve Bulletin* (March 1964), and distribution of savings propensities found in Bureau of Labor Statistics, *Consumer Expenditures and Income, Total United States, Urban and Rural, 1960–61* (Washington, D.C.: Government Printing Office, 1964), p. 304.

14. The excess burdens will be negative for labor since lower incomes lead them to work more.

15. *See* Chapter 3.

16. Bureau of Labor Statistics, *Consumer Expenditures and Income*, BLS Report No. 273. 93, p. 11.

17. Wallace E. Oates, "The Effects of Property Taxes and Local Public Spending on Property Values: An Empirical Study of Tax Capitalization and the Tiebout Hypothesis," *Journal of Political Economy* (November/December 1969), p. 957.

18. For the assumptions used to distribute expenditures, *see Tax Burdens and Benefits of Government Expenditures by Income Class, 1961 and 1965* (New York: Tax Foundation, Inc., 1967).

19. Because of excess burdens, effective tax rates rise as physical wealth holdings rise. Rough calculations of the tax rates of higher income classes can be made using the cross distribution of income and physical wealth.

20. These individuals are assumed to have the average net worth and earned income of individuals in their income class.

21. Board of Governors of Federal Reserve System, "Survey of Financial Characteristics," *Federal Reserve Bulletin* (March, 1964), p. 289.

22. Calculated from production function analysis presented above and data in Table 4-1.

5 Effects on the Level of Economic Activity

Taxes and expenditures may have their most fundamental impacts on an economy's macroeconomic conditions. Unemployment, inflation, and growth all partly depend upon the balance of taxes and expenditures. These three factors in turn all have a major impact on distribution of economic resources. As a consequence this chapter proceeds by first isolating the macroeconomic impacts of different taxes and then isolating the impacts of alternative macroeconomic conditions on the distribution of resources.

Impact Multipliers

To determine the impact of taxes on the level of economic activity, it is necessary to have a complete econometric model of the American economy. Such a model can then be used with different tax systems to simulate the impacts of different types of taxes on the level of economic activity. Since the development, description, justification, and testing of such a model is a book in its own right, such a model will not be presented in this chapter, but the chapter will be based on a model that was developed by the author for the purpose of studying fiscal policies.[1]

The simulation model used three sets of equations. The first set of equations is the supply side of the model. This set of equations calculates the real GNP that would be necessary if the policymaker were to achieve his targets—whatever these targets may be. If the policymaker chooses a target unemployment rate of 4.0 percent after looking at the trade-offs between inflation and unemployment, the supply side of the model is used to calculate the GNP that is compatible with a 4.0 percent unemployment. This is the GNP that would produce a 4.0 percent unemployment rate if it were actually to occur.

To make such calculations the supply side of the model must include labor-force-participation equations and hours-of-work equations to determine the potential labor force. In corresponding fashion it must have investment functions to determine the size of the capital stock, but investment partly depends on after-tax profits from investment. As a consequence, there must be equations to determine profits and profit taxes. Given the equations necessary to determine government employment, the remaining stocks of capital and labor must be inserted into an aggregate production function to determine the supply of private goods and services that would be forthcoming at any definition of full employment.

The second set of equations, the income equations, determine the income flows of governments, corporations, and persons that would be produced by the target (supply side) Gross National Product if it were actually to occur. These income flows are heavily determined by taxes. Of the 14 equations necessary to determine income flows, 8 are tax equations. These include equations for indirect business taxes, income taxes, and social insurance taxes. Thus the tax structure is one of the key ingredients determining the flows of income in the economy. These flows in turn have major impacts on the distribution of economic resources.

The third set of equations, the demand side of the model, estimates the demands for various types of goods and services. There are demand equations for consumption goods, residential investment, inventories, imports, and the private goods and services necessary to produce public goods and services. The key ingredients in these demand equations, however, are the income flows generated in the income side of the model. Since changes in the structure of taxes lead to changes in income flows, they also lead to changes in the structure of demand.

As the model is constructed the summation of each sector's income must necessarily equal the supply-side estimate of GNP.

The demand for goods and services, however, need not equal the supply of goods and services. In Keynesian terms, planned savings at full employment need not equal planned investment. As a result neither the economy nor the model automatically runs at full employment. Whether either is at full employment or not depends on the structure of government tax, expenditures, and monetary policies.

If supply and demand are not equal, the aim of the macro-economic policymaker is to raise or lower the demand for GNP so that it is equal to the supply side (target) GNP. Given a gap, the target unemployment rate cannot be achieved unless government policies are altered. The government may change its own demand for goods and services or alter grants-in-aid, corporate or personal income taxes, indirect business taxes, social insurance taxes, transfer payments, or interest rates so as to change private or state and local demand. Many combinations of these policies are possible; the choice among them must be based on considerations that are outside of the scope of this book.

It should be noted that the gap between the supply and demand estimates of GNP is not the familiar gap calculated in recent reports of the Council of Economic Advisers. The CEA gap is between "potential" GNP—the supply-side GNP—and the actual GNP. The gap in this model is between potential (full employment) GNP and the GNP that would be demanded given the incomes generated by an economy achieving this potential.

The impact of taxes on the gap between the supply-side GNP and the demand-side GNP differs from tax to tax and over time. Different taxes have different effects because they affect the incomes of groups with different propensities to consume or invest. The impacts differ over time because there are lags between changes in incomes and the induced changes in expenditures.

To determine the magnitude of the changes in alternative tax instruments that would be required to bring the demands for goods and services into equilibrium with the supply of goods and services at the target level of unemployment, simulations were run to estimate the magnitude of the changes in taxes that would be required to eliminate a $1 billion gap between the supply estimates of GNP and the demands that would be generated by this GNP.[2] In these simulations each tax is altered separately to provide quantitative estimates of its impact. Table 5-1 presents the first-year effects of simulations in which each policy instrument is altered separately until it is capable of closing a $1 billion gap.[3] For comparative purposes similar simulations were undertaken for federal government purchases (except employee compensation), for federal employee compensation, and for grants-in-aid.

There is a wide range in the effectiveness of these instruments. Only a $0.8 billion change in Government grants-in-aid would be required to fill a gap of $1 billion between supply and demand, but a $3.0 billion change in corporate profits taxes would be required to accomplish the same objective.

Since Federal purchases of goods and services are a direct component of aggregate demand, a $1 billion change in Federal purchases results in a $1 billion change in aggregate demand. Thus the change in Federal purchases necessary to close a gap between the supply and demand estimates of GNP is given by the size of the gap. However, this is not the case for the other policy instruments since they may affect supply as well as demand and since their impact on demand works indirectly via incomes. Table 5-1 shows how alternative policy instruments generate different impacts through their effects on the various elements of supply, income, and demand.

For instance, a cut of $3.0 billion in corporate profits taxes increases corporate incomes by $2.9 billion. This causes an increase of $0.9 billion in corporate investment. The investment increase raises the capital stock and thus increases the supply estimate of GNP by $0.2 billion. With a larger GNP and with higher dividends because of the tax cut, disposable personal income rises $0.4 billion, leading to a rise in personal demand of $0.3 billion. Thus, a $3.0 billion corporate profits tax cut results in a $1.2 billion increase in aggregate demand and a $0.2 billion increase in aggregate supply, eliminating a gap of $1 billion between supply-and-demand GNP.

On the other hand, an increase of $0.8 billion in grants-in-aid to state and local governments decreases potential GNP by

TABLE 5-1[1]

First-Year Effects on Supply, Income, and Demand Resulting from Changes in Government Expenditures and Receipts Necessary to Eliminate a $1 Billion Excess of Supply Estimate of GNP over Demand Estimate

Government Expenditures and Receipts	Change in Government Expenditures and Receipts	Supply Effects: Change in Supply GNP	Income Effects			Demand Effects		
			Change in Disposable Personal Income	Change in Corporate Internal Funds	Net Change in Government Receipts	Change in Personal Demand[2]	Change in Corporate Demand[3]	Change in Government Purchases
Federal Government Purchases (Except Compensation)	$1.0	0	0	0	0	0	0	$1.0
Indirect Business Taxes	-1.8	0	$1.6	0	-$1.6	$1.0	0	0
Corporate Profits Taxes	-3.0	$0.2	0.4	$2.9	-2.9	0.3	$0.9	0
Personal Income Taxes	-1.6	0	1.6	0	-1.6	1.0	0	0
Social Insurance Contributions	-1.8	0	1.6	0	-1.6	1.0	0	0
Federal Employee Compensation	0.9	-0.3	0	-0.1	-0.2	0	-0.2	0.9
Transfer Payment to Persons	1.8	0	1.6	0	0.2	1.0	0	0
Grants-in-Aid	0.8	-0.5	-0.2	-0.1	0.6	-0.1	-0.2	0.8

[1]These data reflect the relative prices and tax structure of the year 1967.

[2]Consists of all demand elements that are dependent upon disposable personal income, i.e., personal consumption expenditures, investments in residential structures, and imports.

[3]Consists of private investment in nonresidential structures, producers' durable equipment, and change in business inventories.

$0.5 billion. This occurs for two reasons. First, an increase in grants-in-aid causes an increase in state and local government employment. The increase in the number of government employees is exactly offset by a decrease in the number of private employees, since the total of private and government employment is fixed by the estimates of the labor force and the target unemployment rate. Since the GNP per private employee is higher than that per government employee, the net effect of this shift in the composition of employment is to decrease the supply-potential GNP. Second, the decrease in private GNP causes a decrease in corporate incomes, which reduces investment and the capital stock and thus further contributes to the reduction in the supply estimate of GNP. The various income changes induced by the increase in grants-in-aid cause a net increase of $0.5 billion in demand, with an $0.8 billion increase in state and local government purchases offset by small declines in personal and corporate demand. Thus, an $0.8 billion increase in grants-in-aid results in a $0.5 billion decrease in aggregate supply and a $0.5 billion increase in aggregate demand, eliminating a gap of $1 billion.

Alternative policy combinations that will eliminate a billion-dollar gap can be calculated by using Table 5-1. For example, the combination of a personal tax cut of $0.8 billion (one-half of $1.6 billion) with an increase in transfer payments of $0.9 billion (one-half of $1.8 billion) would eliminate a gap of $1 billion between supply and demand GNP as would a combined corporate tax cut of $1.5 billion and a personal tax cut of $0.8 billion.

Because of lags in economic reactions, the impact of fiscal policies depends on the time period under consideration. To close annual gaps of equal size over a number of successive years, policies must vary over time. The necessary variations can be seen in Table 5-2. For example, if because of a cut in personal taxes, disposable personal income is increased $1.6 billion in year one, consumption will increase $1.0 billion in that year.[4] However, because both lagged disposable personal income and lagged consumption are explanatory variables in the estimating equation for personal consumption expenditures, the tax changes made in year one will have an $0.2 billion effect on

TABLE 5-2[1]

Change in Government Expenditures and Receipts Necessary to Eliminate a $1 Billion Excess of Supply Estimate of GNP over Demand Estimate

Government Expenditures and Receipts	First Year	Second Year[1]	Third Year[2]
Federal Government Purchases (Except Compensation	$1.0	$1.0	$1.0
Indirect Business Taxes	1.8	1.6	1.4
Corporate Profits Taxes	3.0	1.8	1.6
Personal Income Taxes	1.6	1.3	1.2
Social Insurance Contributions	1.8	1.5	1.3
Federal Employee Compensation	0.9	0.8	0.8
Transfer Payments to Persons	1.8	1.5	1.3
Grants-in-Aid	0.8	0.8	0.8

[1]Lester C. Thurow, "A Fiscal Model of the United States," *Survey of Current Business* (June, 1969) (Washington, D.C.: Government Printing Office), p. 55.

[2]Entries in the second and third columns indicate the change in government expenditures and receipts required in the given year, provided that the changes made for the previous years are those indicated in the previous columns. The data in these columns reflect the relative prices and tax structure of the year 1967.

consumption in year two. The gap that remains to be closed in year two, therefore, is $0.8 billion, rather than the original $1.0 billion, and the tax cut necessary to close this gap in year two is not $1.6 billion, but 80 percent of this amount, or $1.3 billion. In year three, the tax cut made in year one continues to have a small effect on consumption through the influence of the lagged consumption variable. In addition, the $1.3 billion tax cut made in year two affects consumption in year three, through the lagged income and consumption terms. The combined effect on consumption in year three of tax cuts in years one and two is $0.27 billion. Accordingly, we need to fill a gap of only $0.73 billion in year three, and this is accomplished by a personal tax cut of $1.2 billion.

Since not all policy instruments affect the same set of variables, the various fiscal measures differ in their impact over time. For instance, in the case of corporate profits taxes, the successive tax cuts required to fill a gap of $1 billion in each of 3 consecutive

years are \$3.0 billion in year one, followed by \$1.8 billion in year
two, and \$1.6 billion in year three.

Distributional Effects

To isolate the impact of variations in macroeconomic conditions on the distribution of economic resources, a model must be
developed to explain the changes in the distribution of income
caused by macroeconomic factors. Since the impacts on blacks
and whites seem to be different, the model will be disaggregated
to look at the impacts of macroeconomic variables on the
distribution of income for blacks and for whites.

To investigate changes in the American income distribution,
it is necessary to use some technique for describing and manipul-
ating entire distributions. One answer is to fit analytic distributions to the observed distribution of income and then to relate
the parameters of these distributions to macroeconomic variables.

The Beta Distribution. A number of analytic distributions can be
used to describe changes in the distributions of income for
blacks and whites, but the beta distribution seems most desirable.[5]
It fits the observed income distributions well (*see below*), has only
two parameters, and is very flexible. The two parameters are p
and σ (*see* Equation 1). By placing incomes on a scale between 0
and 1, the proportion of the population, p, who have some
particular income is easily calculated (*see* Equation 2). Depending
upon the particular parameters chosen, the beta distribution
can assume a wide variety of shapes.

Complete Beta Function

$$(1) \qquad \beta(\rho, \sigma) = \int_0^1 t^{\rho-1}(1-t)^{\sigma-1}\, dt$$

where
$$\rho > 0$$
$$\sigma > 0$$

$$(2) \qquad f\beta(p\,|\,\rho, v) = \frac{1}{\beta(\rho, \sigma)}\, p^{\rho-1}(1-p)^{\sigma-1}$$

where $\quad 0 \le p \le 1$
$$\sigma = v - \rho$$
$$\rho, \sigma > 0$$

The impact of changes in ρ and σ on the distribution of income is easily determined. Increases in σ (*see* Chart 5-1) result in higher median incomes and smaller relative income differences between the top and bottom of the income distribution. In the ranges under consideration here a 1 percent increase in σ (holding ρ constant) results in an approximately 0.8 percent increase in the median income and a 0.4 percent reduction in the relative income gap between the 25th and 75th percentile of the income distribution. Increases in ρ (*see* Chart 5-2) result in lower median incomes and larger relative income differences in the income distribution. A 1 percent increase in ρ results in a 0.4 percent reduction in the median incomes and a 1 percent increase in the relative income gap between the 25th and 75th percentile of the income distribution. When both ρ and σ rise in the same proportion (*see* Chart 5-3) median incomes remain constant, but relative income differences increase. The dispersing impact of ρ dominates the concentrating impact of σ. More precisely, a 1 percent increase in both ρ and σ results in a 0.2 percent increase in the income gap between the 25th and 75th percentiles of the income distribution.

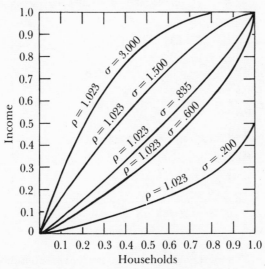

CHART 5-1. Distribution Parameters and the Distribution of Income

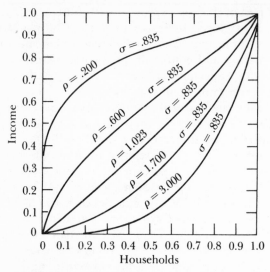

CHART 5-2. Distribution Parameters and the Distribution of Income

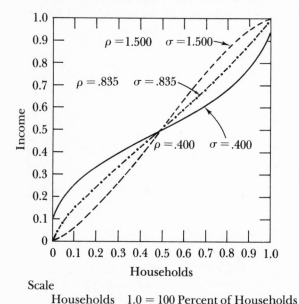

Scale

| Households | 1.0 = 100 Percent of Households |
| Income | 1.0 = $15,000 |

CHART 5-3. Distribution Parameters and the Distribution of Income

Estimating ρ and σ. The beta distribution was fitted to U.S. Bureau of Census constant dollar (1959) income distribution statistics for households (families and unrelated individuals) for every year from 1949 to 1966. Any number of observations could have been used in the estimating process, but ten were actually used. These ten observations were the proportion of the population who had incomes less than 0.05 through 0.95 of the income scale. Since the beta distribution is a finite distribution, it has a maximum income implicit in its estimation. It can be adjusted, but was set here at $15,000. Thus everyone who has an income over $15,000 is given an income of $15,000 for the year of the analysis. This is not a serious constraint, since less than 5 percent of the population have incomes over $15,000 (1959 dollars) in 1966. A $25,000 income limit works just as well, but seemed inappropriate over the period under consideration. The proper income limit depends upon the focus of the analysis. The larger the income limit the more weight is put upon the upper tail of the income distribution in the estimating process.[7] Since the earlier incidence analysis was not able to break incomes above $15,000 into different income classes, the same income limit was used here.

Between 1949 and 1966 the median incomes of white households rose from $3,796 to $6,084 (1959 dollars) and from $1,885 to $3,429 for black households. Measured in terms of Gini coefficients[8] or relative incomes, there have been almost no changes in the distribution of either white or black incomes (*see* Chart 5-4).

The beta distribution fit the actual income distributions well. The coefficient of determination (R^2) improves over the period, but averages 0.96 for whites and 0.92 for blacks (*see* Table 5-3). Rho and sigma rise for both whites and blacks. Median incomes have grown and the dispersion of income has remained relatively constant over the period under consideration, but this was a product of two offsetting forces. Increases in ρ lead to a greater income dispersion and increases in σ lead to less income dispersion. While the distribution impacts of ρ and σ offset each other, the σ dominated ρ in terms of growth in absolute incomes.

The ρ's and σ's differ substantially between blacks and whites. Rho is relatively higher for blacks while sigma is lower, reflecting

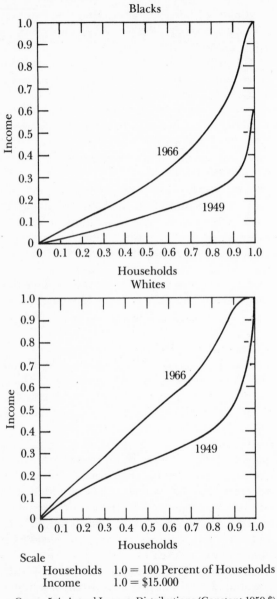

CHART 5-4. Actual Income Distributions (Constant 1959 $)

TABLE 5-3
Time Series Distribution Parameters

	Whites			Blacks		
	ρ	σ	R^2	ρ	σ	R^2
1949	0.666	0.258	0.92	0.930	0.160	0.88
1950	0.687	0.279	0.93	0.930	0.172	0.86
1951	0.625	0.269	0.93	0.908	0.182	0.88
1952	0.649	0.298	0.94	0.921	0.205	0.89
1953	0.667	0.327	0.95	0.920	0.228	0.89
1954	0.697	0.334	0.96	0.929	0.217	0.89
1955	0.718	0.368	0.96	0.913	0.225	0.96
1956	0.731	0.411	0.97	0.978	0.249	0.94
1957	0.728	0.406	0.96	1.025	0.269	0.94
1958	0.750	0.411	0.96	1.075	0.276	0.92
1959	0.765	0.460	0.97	1.051	0.286	0.95
1960	0.815	0.504	0.97	1.061	0.330	0.94
1961	0.979	0.622	0.98	1.173	0.346	0.93
1962	0.971	0.663	0.98	1.107	0.338	0.91
1963	0.985	0.712	0.98	1.073	0.356	0.94
1964	1.017	0.785	0.99	1.095	0.406	0.94
1965	1.029	0.842	0.99	1.124	0.452	0.95
1966	1.044	0.955	0.99	1.104	0.514	0.96

the fact that the income distribution for blacks is much more disperse than that for whites. The same differences can be seen in Gini coefficients. The Gini coefficient for blacks is substantially higher than it is for whites.

Growth of the two parameters is also substantially different. The white ρ rose from 0.666 to 1.044 while the black ρ rose from 0.930 to 1.104. The white σ rose from 0.258 to 0.955 while the black σ rose from 0.160 to 0.514. Thus by the end of the period, the ρ's are rather similar, but the black σ is only half as large as the white σ. Thus most of the differences in income level and dispersion is produced by the σ parameter.

Factors Producing Changes in ρ and σ over Time. In this analysis the impact of macroeconomic factors is separated into five parts. There is a real growth component (measured in terms of constant dollar GNP per employee, GNP/E); an inflation component (measured in terms of the implicit price deflator for

GNP, I); a factor shares component (measured in terms of the share going to personal income, PI/GNP); a utilization component (measured in terms of the proportion of the labor force employed, E/LF); a transfer payment component (measured in terms of the transfer payments per household, TP/H), and a government expenditures component (measured in terms of government purchases of goods and services per household, GP/H).[9] The model is given in Equation 3.[10]

$$(3) \quad \rho \text{ or } \sigma = A \left(\frac{GNP}{E}\right)^{b_0} (I)^{b_1} \left(\frac{PI}{GNP}\right)^{b_2} \left(\frac{E}{LF}\right)^{b_3} \left(\frac{TP}{H}\right)^{b_4} \left(\frac{GP}{H}\right)^{b_5} e$$

where
A = intercept
GNP = gross national product
E = total employment
I = implicit price deflator for GNP
PI = personal income
LF = total labor force
TP = transfer payments
H = households
GP = government purchases of goods and services
$b_0 \ldots b_1$ = elasticities

The results of estimating Equation 3 are given in Table 5-4. Whenever variables had t-statistics less than 1, that variable was dropped from the model. The same variable can, of course, be instrumental in explaining both ρ and σ. Growth can lead to both a more dispersed and a more concentrated income distribution. To determine the net impact of growth on the income distribution, its impact on the two parameters must be combined. Thus for whites the elasticity of ρ with respect to GNP/E is 1.20 and the elasticity of σ with respect to GNP/E is 2.94. Since the income-dispersing effect of ρ is roughly twice as large as the income-concentrating effect of σ, the income-dispersing effects cancel each other (*see above*). Growth leads to higher real incomes, but does not have any major impact on the dispersion of income.

The rate of inflation also has two conflicting tendencies for whites. A 1 percent increase in inflation results in a 1.55 percent reduction in ρ and a 0.64 percent reduction in σ. Reductions in ρ lead to a more concentrated income distribution and reduction

TABLE 5-4[1]
Time Series Distribution Elasticities

		White		Black	
		ρ	σ	ρ	σ
A		3.97	−3.24	−1.47	0.05
		(2.44)	(2.21)	(0.93)	(0.50)
GNP/E	b_0	1.20	2.94	−0.73	
		(0.60)	(0.43)	(0.18)	
I	b_1	−1.55	−0.64	0.68	
		(0.57)	(0.55)	(0.23)	
PI/GNP	b_2	−2.43			1.56
		(1.50)			(1.18)
E/LF	b_3	−2.52			6.23
		(1.94)			(1.37)
TP/H	b_4	0.49	0.39	0.26	0.73
		(0.22)	(0.13)	(0.07)	(0.06)
GP/H	b_5				0.37
					(0.08)
Correlation Coefficient		0.96	0.99	0.95	0.99
Standard Error of Estimate		0.04	0.05	0.02	0.04
Durbin-Watson		1.82	1.59	2.13	2.05
Degrees of Freedom		12	14	14	13

[1]Standard errors in parenthesis.

in σ leads to more dispersed income distribution. Since the ρ effects are roughly twice as powerful as the σ effects in terms of income dispersion, inflation seems to be a powerful force leading to a more equal *real* distribution of income.

The offsetting impacts of business cycles on white incomes can be seen in the PI/GNP and E/LF terms. In booms, employment rises but the proportion of income going to persons falls. Rising employment leads to a lower ρ and more equality, but a falling share for personal income leads to a rising ρ and more inequality. Because of these two offsetting forces the distribution of white income does not change markedly over the course of a business cycle.

Transfer payments present a bit of a problem for whites. They have an impact on both ρ and σ, but the results indicate that increasing transfer payments leads to a greater dispersion of incomes for whites. Since most government transfer payments do not go to the very rich or the very poor such a result is not impossible, but it is surprising. For whites, government pensions, veterans' benefits, and social security benefits to the middle class dominate welfare payments to the poor.[11]

Such is not the case for blacks. Transfer payments influence both ρ and σ, but the impact on σ is three times as large as that on ρ. Consequently transfer payments lead to a more equal distribution of black income. Given the size of central-city welfare payments such a result is not surprising.

Government purchases of goods and services lead to higher and more equal black incomes whereas they have no impact on the level or distribution of white incomes. Direct and indirect employment on government projects is one of the major causes of increases in black incomes.

Business cycles have conflicting impacts on the level and distribution of black incomes, but the impacts do not balance out as they did for whites. The employment elasticity (b_3) is four times as large as the share elasticity (b_2). Full employment is a powerful force leading to higher black incomes and more equal black incomes since blacks suffer more than their share of unemployment and consequently are differentially aided by its elimination.

Inflation, however, leads to more unequal black incomes. Instead of being negatively related to ρ as it is for whites, inflation is positively related to ρ for blacks. Since black incomes are almost entirely wage and salary earnings and since rich blacks are lower middle class by white standards, these results may simply indicate that the incomes of those people who are lower middle class by white standards rise relatively in inflationary periods. Thus, if inflation and employment are related to each other as in the Phillips' curve, part of the equalizing impact of full employment will be offset by the concomitant inflation, though employment elasticity is almost 9 times as large as the inflation elasticity. Adjusting for the differences in the impact of ρ and σ on the distribution of income still means that there is a powerful equalizing impact from full employment.

General growth has a different impact on black and white

incomes. Growth (GNP/E) is negatively related to the black ρ parameter rather than being positively related to both ρ and σ as for whites. For whites, growth leads to higher incomes but does not have much, if any, net impact on the distribution of income. For blacks, growth leads to higher real incomes, but it also leads to more equal incomes. This occurs since black incomes, rich and poor, are dependent on wage and salary earnings. Thus the growth of capital incomes that prevents growth from equalizing white incomes does not affect black incomes.

Conclusions

The analysis in this chapter indicates that different taxes and expenditures have different impact multipliers. This fact, as mentioned earlier, makes it impossible to do standard differential incidence studies. The substitute of alternative taxes that yield the same revenue is not a method of eliminating macroeconomic effects.

Of all the distribution effects of macroeconomic variables, the conclusion that inflation causes the income distribution to become more equal is probably the most surprising to the layman. There is no doubt that inflation causes horizontal inequalities (two people with the same real income before a period of inflation may have very different real incomes after a period of inflation), but horizontal inequalities occur throughout the income distribution. They affect rich widows and orphans just as they affect poor widows and orphans. In any case these horizontal inequalities are dominated by vertical equalization. Since low unemployment and inflation seem to go together in the American economy, the resource-equalizing effects of tight labor markets are substantial.

Notes

1. Lester C. Thurow, "A Fiscal Policy Model of the United States," *Survey of Current Business* (June 1969) (Washington, D.C.: Government Printing Office).
2. There are a variety of methods for summarizing the impact of taxes on macroeconomic variables. One method calculates the changes in the Gross National Product that will be produced by a given change in taxes. Another method calculates the changes in taxes that would be necessary to change the

Gross National Product by some specified amount. Impact multipliers of this type will be presented here. Although the results may look different, they are just opposite sides of the same coin—knowing one type of impact, it is easy to calculate the other type of impact.

3. These simulations were undertaken for 1967 and thus reflect the relative prices and tax structure prevailing in that year.

4. Actually, the impact on personal demand is not solely on consumption. There are also minor impacts on imports and residential investment. For the sake of simplicity, the effects of the import and residential investment equations have been ignored in this explanation.

5. For a more detailed discussion of the beta function see M. G. Kendall and A. Stuart, *The Advanced Theory of Statistics* (London, Charles Griffin and Co., 1963), p. 150.

6. The income data are from U.S. Bureau of the Census, *Trends in the Income of Families and Persons in the United States, 1947 to 1960*, USGPO, Table 11; U.S. Bureau of the Census, *Current Population Reports, Consumer Income*, Series P-60, various issues (Washington, D.C.: Government Printing Office).

7. As the maximum income limit increases, the number of upper income observations used in estimating ρ and σ increases.

8. The Gini coefficient is the area between the diagonal and the Lorenze curve divided by the area under the diagonal.

9. These data are standard National Income and Products Account data and standard labor-force data taken from U.S. Department of Labor, *Employment and Earnings*. The employment rate is not the normal unemployment rate since it is total employment divided by the total labor force rather than civilian employment divided by the civilian labor force.

10. The first four terms in this equation yield current dollar percent income per member of the labor force.

$$\left(\frac{GNP}{E}\right)\left(\frac{PI}{GNP}\right)(I)\left(\frac{E}{LF}\right) = \frac{PI}{LF}$$

11. In 1968 government transfer payments totaled $48.6 billion. Direct relief was only $4.9 billion.

6 Variations in State and Local Tax Structures

Up to this point the analysis of tax impacts has treated state and local taxes as if each state and locality had the average state and local tax structure. Since the range of tax structures around the average is large, and since states and localities collect one-third of total government tax revenue, geographical differences cannot ultimately be ignored. They are one of the major factors affecting the distribution of economic resources.

Before it is possible to determine the significance of local differences in tax structure, however, it is necessary to analyze the nature and goals of fiscal federalism. What are the national goals with respect to state and local expenditures and taxes? How far does society want to decentralize the equity decisions and interpersonal comparisons necessary to collect taxes and make expenditures? What are the national responsibilities to offset differences in economic resources from region to region? No tax program or set of tax programs can be labeled adequate or inadequate without knowing the national targets that are to be achieved. Thus the first part of this chapter is devoted to an analysis of national goals regarding state and local government taxes and expenditures.

Any evaluation of proposed solutions, such as the Nixon revenue-sharing proposals of 1969, needs to know society's desired targets, but it also needs to know the current situation with respect to these targets. The second part of this chapter is therefore devoted to analysis of the current situation. When national targets, the current local situation, and suggested federal programs are compared, the suggested programs are inadequate in solving the problems state and local tax collectors create.[1] It might be expected that they would be inadequate with respect to size, but they are also incapable of reaching national objectives regardless of the amount of money that is devoted to them. The programs (instruments) are simply too few in number relative to national objectives (targets).[2]

Since adequate solutions lie far outside the boundaries or present discussions, the boundaries of the discussion must be widened. To do this the final section focuses on the nature of the solutions as well as the technical problems, that would be necessary to reach society's objectives.

The Federal Perspective

Federal systems of government are established because decentralized decision-making is both a means to efficient and equitable government and an end in its own right. Although decentralization is an end in its own right, decentralization is not the fundamental purpose of government. If it were, America would break up into many small countries, and our ideal would be "each man his own government." Moreover, if decentralization were the only goal, we would not be talking about Federal aid to state and local governments. We would demand that each government raise its own revenue.

Equity and efficiency are at least coequal goals with decentralization. Unavoidable clashes between equity, efficiency, and decentralization lead to the Federal interests in state and local government tax and expenditure decisions. These clashes spring from three sources—externalities, the national need to establish vertical and horizontal equity among its citizens, and merit wants.

Externalities. External economies or diseconomies are associated with many of the functions that have been delegated to state and local governments. One jurisdiction's actions have positive or negative benefits for individuals living in other jurisdictions. Some benefits are exported directly to other parts of the country (pollution, etc), and other benefits are exported indirectly through outmigration (education, etc.). Education, health, sewerage, and possibly welfare constitute the state and local programs that have the largest impact on other parts of the country, but many other activities could have substantial external effects. Thus, for example, a lack of public parks in one area could create negative benefits (costs) for other areas if the lack of local parks leads residents of this area to use parks in other areas, or if it leads to frustrated or angry outmigration because of the lack of local public services. Depriving individuals of public services in one part of the country adversely affects individuals in other parts of the country.

With externalities no set of purely local decisions can lead to the proper amount of public services. Each government unit will expand its public services to the point at which the local marginal benefits from these services are equal to the local marginal costs of these services. If some of the benefits accrue to individuals in other areas, or if the programs create costs for individuals in other areas, these benefits or costs will be rightly ignored by the local decision-makers. Each unit of government will think it is being efficient, but the totality of decisions will be inefficiency. Neither national or local efficiency will in fact be achieved. For national efficiency, programs must be expanded in each area until national marginal benefits equal national marginal costs. Ignoring spillouts and spillins could lead to either over- or underproduction of local public services, but in general it probably leads to underproduction.

If efficient national decisions are to be made, some mechanism must be found to make each local government respond to national benefits and costs, rather than local benefits and costs. The only method for doing this is a system of Federal fiscal incentives that modify local benefits and costs so that they are equal to national benefits and costs.

Consequently, any system of Federal aid to state and local governments must be capable of modifying local benefits and costs for functions with externalities so that they are equal to national benefits and costs. This, then, is the first of the ingredients that must go into a Federal system of optimum taxation.

Horizontal and Vertical Equity. Presumably, one of the functions of government is to insure vertical and horizontal equity among its *citizens.* Equals are to be treated equally, and society is to achieve its optimum distribution of real income (income includes public and private goods and services). In welfare economics the definition of equality and the optimum distribution of income are contained in the social-welfare function. But who should determine the social-welfare function — the national government, state governments, or local governments? Or is there some way to decentralize the determination of the social-welfare function? This is the fundamental question of fiscal federalism.

Decentralized determination of the social-welfare function means that different areas will have different definitions of equity. The definition of equity in an area will be a weighted composite of the equity decisions of each level of government that affects it. What is horizontally and vertically equitable in one place will be inequitable in another. Thus the possibilities of decentralization revolve around whether a society can or should operate with different definitions of equity for different groups of its citizens. The answer to this question is partly a matter of taste and partly a matter of analysis.

The question of taste revolves around individual preferences. Are Americans interested in "fair" treatment for every citizen of the United States, or are they only interested in "fair" treatment for citizens in their own local area? Are they willing to let each local area choose its own optimum distribution of income? Should one area be allowed to opt for complete equality (equal incomes for each individual), while another area opts for complete inequality (all income for one man)? Has horizontal equity been achieved when individuals in poor areas must pay higher tax rates to gain exactly the same public services that individuals with the same income in wealthy areas obtain with low tax rates, or are we only interested in equal treatment of equals within each local area?

To pose these questions is to answer them. Most Americans may be more interested in what happens in their own area than in the country at large, but they are interested in achieving some measure of horizontal and vertical equity in other areas. The degree of interest is not important for our purposes because as long as they have any interest a federal system of taxation must be capable of modifying or constraining state and local equity decisions. Whether the system is in fact used to equalize state and local equity decisions across the country is a subsidiary question.

Analysis points in the same direction. Standards of vertical and horizontal equity can themselves produce externalities. A wide dispersion in real standards of living both within and among areas may produce crime, social unrest, political unrest, and a host of other social and private ailments. If such is the case (and there is a general presumption that it is the case for wide dispersions) the problem of externalities mentioned above becomes relevant for efficient selection of equity standards. Each local government will choose the definition of equity that maximizes its own local welfare, but with externalities the summation of such decisions will not yield the maximum amount of national or local welfare. Maximizing the national and local welfare received from achieving equity requires some overall coordination of equity standards.

In addition to the problem of horizontal and vertical equity within regions there is the problem of horizontal and vertical equity between regions. Does society have a desired national income distribution for each region? If it has achieved its desired national distribution of income, should it move to equalize incomes among areas? Does it care whether the rich and poor live separately or together? Answers to all of these questions are necessary before it is possible to say whether society should have a policy of equalizing economic resources between regions.

To some extent, however, it is possible to separate the distributions of private incomes and public incomes (public goods and services received). Society may not be worried about equalizing income distributions among areas as long as it has achieved its desired national distribution of income, but still be worried about equalizing the ability to purchase public goods and services. It may simply think that public goods should be more equally distributed than private goods. If this is the case, the tax system needs to be able to equalize potential public purchases even if it is not equalizing potential private purchases.

Consequently, a federal structure of taxes must be capable of modifying and constraining local definitions of vertical and horizontal equity, but it also must be capable of achieving horizontal and vertical equity among its region. This, then, is the second of the ingredients that must go into a federal tax structure.

Merit Wants. Some state and local public services fall into a category of what are called merit wants.[3] Merit wants are goods that society decides are so important that some minimum quantity is regarded as a fundamental right. Education is the prime example. In a society dedicated to equal opportunities for each individual, some minimum quantity of education may be part of each individual's fundamental rights. Just as an equal opportunity is part of his fundamental rights. In our society education is so important that we regard some minimum quantity as both a right and a duty. Individuals are forced by law to attend school for some minimum period of time. Although there would be less agreement, adequate health care and housing may be other examples of merit wants.

Merit wants are connected with equity decisions, but they involve a different aspect of equity than horizontal and vertical equity. Horizontal and vertical equity goals involve making sure that each individual has the income that society thinks he should have. The desired income level may be his market earnings or some other income. Society provides merit wants in order that its citizens may be treated equitably, but it does not allow the individual to choose whether he wants these goods. They are distributed directly in terms of services, rather than as part of the general distribution of economic resources.

Merit wants can arise for a number of reasons. They may simply be goods that society wants to distribute more equally than goods in general. If the distribution of income were allowed to determine their distribution, they would be too unequally distributed. They may be goods that are necessary for noneconomic aspects of our national lives—i.e., good political decision-making in a democracy. Whatever the reason, they constitute a class of goods by which society wants to guarantee that each individual in society will have some minimum quantity.

Consequently, a Federal tax structure must be capable of insuring that each individual receives his minimum quantity of merit wants. This, then, is the third of the ingredients that must go into a Federal system.

What, then, are the ingredients of an adequate system of Federal taxation? It must insure that each person receives at least the specified minimum quantity of merit wants, it must modify local benefits and costs so that they are equal to national benefits and costs for those goods with externalities, and it must constrain local equity decisions within the range of acceptable national definitions of vertical and horizontal equity. Within these constraints it should preserve the maximum possible amount of decentralization.

Achieving the three national goals listed above still leaves local governments with a wide variety of important decisions. Except for minimum quantities of merit wants and the modifications required by externalities, local governments must find their own positions of social balance. They must decide at what point the marginal benefits from public expenditures are equal to the marginal benefits of private expenditures (the marginal costs of public expenditures) for total expenditures and for specific expenditures. Even with goods that have externalities, much of the decision-making power is left with local governments. Fiscal incentives are arranged so that local governments will find it profitable to add national benefits and costs to their local benefits and costs, but the local government still determines local benefits and costs. If the local government is spending more than the required minimum amount on merit wants, even marginal decisions about merit wants come under the domain of the local government. Thus, decentralized decision-making is not an empty concept, even when the national goals are being fulfilled.

The Current Situation

Before going on to examine the adequacy of proposed solutions, it is necessary to see how close the present system comes to achieving the three national goals outlined above. Merit wants and goods with externalities can be looked at together since in each case there is some minimum quantity of these goods required in the national interest. Exactly what this minimum is depends upon society's national social-welfare function. Although these goals have not been spelled out clearly enough for an economist to calculate the necessary minimum quantities of each of these goods, the present dispersions in the expenditures on different local services at least create prima-facie evidence that these minimums are *not* being reached (*see* Table 6-1).

TABLE 6-1[1]
State and Local Expenditures per Capita
in 1966–67

		Range	
Function	Average	High	Low
Education	$193	$322	$133
Local Schools	142	242	89
Higher Education	45	109	3
Highways	71	438	49
Public Welfare	42	84	15
Health and Hospitals	36	81	15
Police	15	42	7
Fire	8	19	2
Sewerage	8	18	2
Sanitation Other Than Sewerage	5	12	1
Parks and Recreation	7	20	1

[1]U.S. Bureau of the Census, *Government Finances in 1966–67* (Washington, D.C.: Government Printing Office, 1968), pp. 45–48.

It is doubtful that the 1966–1967 per capita expenditures of $89 on local schools, $3 on higher education, $15 on welfare, $15 on health and hospitals, $2 on sewerage, $1 on sanitation other than sewerage, and $1 on parks and recreation in the lowest-expenditure state are high enough to yield the desired national benefits for those goods that have externalities or high enough to constitute acceptable minimum standards for merit wants. These expenditures are simply too low in comparison with national averages or with the highest-expenditure states. The range of the dispersions at least creates a presumptive case that Federal aid programs need to be able to influence expenditures on goods with externalities and upon merit wants.

Dispersions in equity standards are harder to determine since each local government should have the right to determine its own position of social balance. High relative tax rates, therefore, do not indicate inequities since they may be offset by high relative expenditures. High tax rates may simply indicate a preference for public goods. This means some equity standard that takes into account both expenditures and effort must be constructed.

Tax effort is generally measured in terms of revenue collected per $1,000 of personal income. Such an effort index ignores the Federal government poverty line, a line that specifies the minimum *private* income that each individual should receive. Consequently, effort should be measured in terms of tax collections per dollar of income above the poverty line. One method of doing this is to calculate the revenue collected per $1,000 of personal income above $800 per capita. The per capita poverty line for families of four is approximately $800 per capita.

Such an effort index indicated a range from $273 in Mississippi to $132 in Illinois, with an average of $180 (*see* Table 6-2). Mississippi's effective tax rate (27.3 percent) is more than twice as high as that of Illinois (13.2 percent). It is interesting to note the low-effort states. They read like a roll of wealthy states: Connecticut, $138; D.C., $124; Illinois, $132; New Jersey, $144, and Ohio, $143.

Before equity judgments can be made, however, benefits must be brought into the calculus. The simplest way to do this is to look at per capita expenditures. In 1966–1967 state and local governments spent $474 per capita, but expenditures ranged from $1,198 in Alaska to $305 in South Carolina (*see* Table 6-2). If Alaska is left aside because of the peculiar role of the Federal government in that state, Wyoming is the highest expenditure state, with expenditures of $749. Wyoming spent approximately $2½ per capita for every dollar spent in South Carolina, and Alaska spent almost four dollars for every dollar spent in South Carolina.

Per Capita Expenditures per Dollar of State and Local Revenue per

| State | General Expenditures Per Capita | | State and Local Revenue[2] | $1 \div 3$ | $2 \div 3$ |
| | *Current* | *Deflated* | | | |
	(1)	(2)	(3)	(4)	(5)
Alabama	360	501	206	1.7	2.4
Alaska	1,198	905	201	6.0	4.5
Arizona	523	477	236	2.2	2.0
Arkansas	339	527	211	1.6	2.5
California	651	491	194	3.4	2.5
Colorado	539	557	214	2.5	2.6
Connecticut	472	400	138	3.4	2.9
Delaware	607	593	175	3.5	3.4
D.C.	593	532	124	4.8	4.3
Florida	435	463	205	2.1	2.3
Georgia	375	468	191	2.0	2.5
Hawaii	667	623	217	3.1	2.9
Idaho	453	539	234	1.9	2.3
Illinois	418	387	132	3.2	2.9
Indiana	412	387	170	2.4	2.3
Iowa	477	531	187	2.6	2.8
Kansas	440	492	191	2.3	2.6
Kentucky	410	529	198	2.1	2.7
Louisiana	485	516	240	2.0	2.2
Maine	414	501	190	2.2	2.6
Maryland	473	432	167	2.8	2.6
Massachusetts	466	429	171	2.7	2.5
Michigan	510	482	168	3.0	2.9
Minnesota	547	925	216	2.5	2.4
Mississippi	346	552	273	1.3	2.0
Missouri	404	439	162	2.5	2.7
Montana	509	562	211	2.4	2.7

6-2[1]

$1,000 of Personal Income Above $800 per Capita in 1966–67

	General Expenditures Per Capita		State and Local Revenue[2]	$1 \div 3$	$2 \div 3$
	Current	Deflated			
State	(1)	(2)	(3)	(4)	(5)
Nebraska	439	531	169	2.6	3.1
Nevada	700	672	194	3.6	3.5
New Hampshire	406	468	157	2.6	3.0
New Jersey	417	373	144	2.9	2.6
New Mexico	560	547	253	2.2	2.2
New York	615	498	203	3.0	2.5
North Carolina	343	389	191	1.8	2.0
North Dakota	584	681	272	2.1	2.5
Ohio	393	398	143	2.7	2.8
Oklahoma	466	514	212	2.2	2.4
Oregon	538	508	200	2.7	2.5
Pennsylvania	411	412	155	2.7	2.7
Rhode Island	495	441	155	3.2	2.8
South Carolina	305	413	200	1.5	2.1
South Dakota	493	656	228	2.2	2.9
Tennessee	386	528	190	2.0	2.8
Texas	385	401	175	2.2	2.3
Utah	517	551	220	2.4	2.5
Vermont	526	623	206	2.6	3.0
Virginia	380	452	167	2.3	2.7
Washington	557	514	193	2.9	2.7
West Virginia	401	510	202	2.0	2.5
Wisconsin	520	522	197	2.6	2.6
Wyoming	749	763	257	2.9	3.0
Total	474	474	180	2.6	2.6

[1]U.S. Bureau of the Census, *Government Finances in 1966–67* (Washington, D.C.: Government Printing Office, 1968), pp. 45–48, 50, 52.

[2]Per $1,000 of personal income above $800 per capita.

Money differentials do not, of course, automatically mean corresponding real differences in the quantity of public goods and services produced. Costs of producing public services may differ from state to state. Since there are no good deflators for the costs of producing public goods and services in different states, there is no easy or accurate way to correct for price differentials.

The data in Column 2 of Table 6-1 indicate a rough attempt to adjust for price differentials using the median salary of full-time local school teachers as an index of cost differences between states.[4] Teachers' salaries were chosen as the index because teachers' salaries in particular and wages in general represent a large fraction of state and local government expenditures, and because the quality standards for what constitute a teacher are more homogeneous across the different states than the quality standards for other types of employees.

Using teacher's salaries as a deflator overcorrects for price differences for a number of reasons. Teachers in low expenditure states typically have less education than teachers in high expenditure states. Thus wage differentials partially reflect real quality differences, rather than just price differences. Although wages are an important part of state and local government expenditures, they constitute only 50 percent of total expenditures. Many goods purchased by state and local governments are nationally marketed with common prices for all states and localities. Using teachers' salaries as a deflator assumes that all goods are correspondingly cheaper in states with low salaries and higher in states with high salaries. Such is not the case. Wage differentials consequently exaggerate price differentials for goods purchased by state and local governments.

Thus the data in Column 2 of Table 6-2 represent an outer limit. Accurate deflation would not reduce the dispersion in expenditures per capita any further, and in all probability accurate deflators would yield much more dispersion than that exhibited in Column 2. The dispersion is still large. Alaska and Wyoming are still the high expenditure states with expenditures of $905 and $763, but the low expenditure states are now Connecticut with $400 per capita and Texas with $401 per capita.

Connecticut is a low expenditure state with relatively high costs, while Texas is a low expenditure state with about average costs. Instead of having a range of 4 to 1 or $2\frac{1}{2}$ to 1, the range in per capita expenditures is now 2.3 to 1 or 1.9 to 1. Using Wyoming as the base, the dispersion is reduced by approximately 20 percent, but it is still large.

When benefits (expenditures per capita) and effort (taxes per $1,000 of personal income above $800 per capita) are put together in a benefit-effort ratio, the dispersions in each component are compounded. Leaving both Alaska and the District of Columbia aside because of the special role of the Federal government in these areas, money benefit-effort ratios vary from 3.6 in Nevada to 1.3 in Mississippi, with a standard deviation of 0.8. A $2\frac{1}{2}$-to-1 range in expenditures per capita and a 2-to-1 range in effort produces a 2.8-to-1 range in benefit-effort ratios. Using deflated expenditure data, the range is from 3.5 in Nevada, to 2.0 in Arizona and Mississippi. In either case there is a substantial variation in benefit effort ratios between states, even after the present set of federal government aid programs have been taken into account.

The variations within states are just as large or larger than the variations between states. Table 6-3 presents the pertinent data on the variations in county benefit-effort ratios for local governments

TABLE 6-3[1]
Variations in County Benefit-Effort Indices
in 1962

State	Average	High	Low	Standard Deviation
Delaware	1.6	1.8	1.2	0.3
California	1.0	1.5	0.7	0.2
Nevada	1.0	1.3	0.6	0.2
Mississippi	−0.2	0.7	−1.9	0.6
Arkansas	−0.3	2.0	−1.7	0.5
South Carolina	−0.9	0.8	−28.6	4.8

[1]U.S. Bureau of the Census, *Census of Governments, 1962* (Washington, D.C.: Government Printing Office), volumes for Nevada, Delaware, California, Mississippi, Arkansas, and South Carolina.

for the three states with the highest benefit-cost ratios (Nevada, Delaware, and California) and the three states with the lowest benefit-effort ratios. The range in benefit-effort ratios between the highest and lowest county in each state are 1.3 to 0.6, 1.8 to 1.2, 0.7 to −1.9, 2.0 to −1.7, and 0.8 to −28.6. Benefit-effort ratios are negative when per capita incomes are less than $800 per capita. Assuming that the benefit of state expenditures are evenly spread across each state, these data indicate a range of 4.4 to −27.6 in the benefit-effort ratios between the highest benefit-effort county in the three highest benefit-effort states to the lowest benefit-effort expenditure county in the three lowest benefit-effort states.[5] Compounding the problem even further, benefit-effort ratios in high expenditure counties in low expenditure states are often higher than benefit-effort ratios in low expenditure counties in high expenditure states. If it were possible to look at within-county variations in expenditures and tax effort, the dispersion would, of course, be even larger than the 4.4 to −27.6 benefit-effort range calculated above.

Fundamentally, however, variations in benefit-effort indices among areas are irrelevant. The real problem is variations in benefit-effort indices among individuals. The goal is equity among individuals, not among areas. Geographic inequities are only interesting to the extent that they indicate inequities among individuals. Geographic inequities need to be eliminated only because that is a necessary condition for eliminating inequities among individuals.

Variations in benefit-effort indices, however, are only half of the equity problem. They indicate whether horizontal equity (equal treatment of equals) has been achieved, but they do not indicate whether vertical equity (the optimum distribution of income) has been achieved. Vertical equity might be ignored in the present context, however, society can use the Federal tax system achieve vertical equity if state and local governments are horizontally equitable. The Federal government simply builds the desired degree of progression into its tax structure and sets this structure on top of state and local taxes. If states and localities do not achieve horizontal equity, however, there is no way to use the present Federal tax system to achieve either horizontal equity or vertical equity.

The Necessary Ingredients

1. The Federal government wants to insure some minimum quantity of merit wants in each state. Since each state may have different price or income elasticities of demand with respect to merit want goods or services, there is no method of using general unrestricted grants or general matching grants to obtain the desired quantities. A different grant scheme would need to be tailored to the relevant elasticities of each state and locality to reach the desired targets. Consequently, the Federal government must agree to pay 100 percent of the costs of the minimum quantity of merit wants. In no other way is it possible to use general fiscal controls to reach the desired targets. Thus one of the necessary ingredients of an adequate system of Federal taxes must be lump-sum block grants (negative taxes) to state and local governments for those purposes that are considered merit wants.

2. Externalities require a different type of Federal assistance. The Federal government must decide what fraction of the benefits from these goods are national benefits and what fraction are local benefits. Based on this decision it must then set up a system of matching grants (matching negative taxes). Thus, if 50 percent of the benefits from sewerage and sanitation were national benefits, the Federal government would agree to match local expenditures on a 1-for-1 basis.

3. Finally, the Federal government must pick the benefit-effort ratio that it is going to use to equalize around. When the government sets this ratio it will influence the total level of state and local government expenditures, since the magnitude of state and local expenditures will partly depend upon the state the local effort necessary per dollar of expenditures. Given that state and local public services are superior goods, the higher the chosen benefit-effort index, the larger expenditures will be. Consequently, the Federal government should choose a benefit-effort level that it believes will generate on average the proper amount of local public services to obtain social balance (marginal benefits from public goods equal to the marginal benefits from private goods). In any case, equalization means a set of grants (or taxes) made on the basis of both per capita expenditures and local income levels.

Knowing the subsidy system, each state would notify the Federal government of its expenditures per capita. Based on these expenditures and local incomes, the Federal government would then tell the state the size of the per capita grant it would receive or the size of the per capita tax it must pay. In many states, equalization taxes would have the effect of recouping some or all of the money contributed to the states in terms of lump-sum block grants or matching grants. In some states equalization grants would be positive and a source of additional revenue and in other states they would be negative and thus constitute additional Federal taxes. Thus the gross flows of aid might be much larger than the net flows.

The important thing to remember is that if the nation has three national goals, it must have at least three independent policy instruments for achieving these goals. Without at least three independent policy instruments, it will simply be unable to reach each goal.

To illustrate how the system would work and the magnitude of the necessary Federal expenditures, assume that education expenditures of $193 per capita (the 1966–1967 national average) are regarded as a merit want; expenditures on health and hospitals, sewerage and sanitation, public welfare, and parks and recreation are goods with externalities, 50 percent of the benefits of which are national benefits; and that the Federal government decided to equalize benefit-effort ratios at 2.6 (the 1966–1967 national average).

Achieving the desired minimum expenditures on education would require a lump-sum block grant of $38 billion per year for education. The expenditures on Federal matching grants for the goods with externalities would depend upon the price elasticities of demand for these goods. Other evidence indicates that state and local governments on average increase their expenditures by $1 for every $1 in grants-in-aid.[6] Since states and localities now average $96 per capita, for health and hospitals ($34), sewerage and sanitation ($13), public welfare ($42), and parks and recreation ($7), 50–50 matching grants would increase expenditures on these goods to $192 per capita. The aggregate cost of this to the Federal government would be $19 billion dollars.

Assuming that the government is equalizing expenditures at the current benefit-effort ratio of 2.6, however, means that some of the Federal grants of $57 billion ($38 billion plus $19 billion) will be recouped. Exactly how much will be recouped depends upon the expenditure response elasticities with respect to benefit-effort ratios for those states with above average benefit-effort ratios and those states with below average benefit-effort ratios. If the two sets of elasticities are the same, total state and local government expenditures will not change, but they will fall in high benefit-effort states and rise in low benefit-effort states. In aggregate, expenditures would rise by $8.6 billion in one set of states and fall by the same amount in another set of states. To accomplish this would require a proportional equalization tax based on personal income per capita above $800 per capita. In aggregate, the tax would raise $60 billion, distribute $3 billion to the below average benefit-effort states, and return $57 billion to the Federal treasury. Federal tax collection would completely cover Federal grants. The results would be average per capita expenditures of $474 and an equalization of benefit-effort ratios at 2.6. The composition of expenditures would change, however, each state would spend at least $193 per capita on education, and average expenditures on the goods with externalities would rise from $96 per capita to $192 per capita. Expenditures on other public services would drop. The dispersion in expenditures on goods with externalities would depend upon the distribution of price elasticities of demand among different states and localities.

Equalization at higher benefit-effort levels would require large positive contributions. If benefit-effort levels were to be raised from 2.6 to 3.6 (the highest current rate, except for Alaska and the District of Columbia), average per capita expenditures would rise to $654[7] and the Federal government would need to contribute $35 billion to the equalization scheme for distribution to every state except Nevada (the state which currently has a benefit-effort ratio of 3.6).

Existing or Proposed Federal Programs

Suggested or actual aid programs include specific grants-in-aid, block grants-in-aid, unrestricted grants-in-aid, tax credits or deductions for state and local tax payments, and tax-free bonds. Sometimes these programs are used alone, sometimes in conjunction with matching formula or effort indices. Most of these instruments can be rejected as appropriate policy instruments, however, because they do not and cannot help society achieve its national targets.

Specific grants-in-aid can focus expenditures on particular projects, but they are unacceptable because they are dominated by block grants-in-aid. Block grants accomplish the national goals while preserving more decentralized decision-making authority. Tax credits dominate tax deductions for state and local tax payments because of equity considerations, but tax credits are in turn dominated by unrestricted grants. Tax credits would probably have to be given to the individuals who have the legal liability to pay state and local taxes, yet the study of tax incidence indicates that the ultimate tax payer is often not the legal tax payer. Thus, tax credits double the inequities produced by shifting tax incidence. One man is able to shift a tax to someone else, and then gain a tax credit for a tax he did not pay. Consequently, unrestricted grants dominate tax credit. Tax free municipal bonds are simply inefficient (some of the revenue goes to the bond holders, rather than the local governments) and can be used to achieve none of the national targets.

This leaves lump-sum block grants-in-aid, block grants-in-aid used in conjunction with matching formulae, and unrestricted grants-in-aid. The first two are adequate instruments to simultaneously achieve the desired minimum quantities of merit wants and to reflect the national benefits produced by local expenditures with externalities, but unrestricted grants-in-aid are not in general adequate as an equalization instrument. First, unrestricted grants-in-aid must be used in conjunction with a benefit-effort index. They cannot be given out on a per capita basis or on the basis of tax collections alone. They must be given out based on a formula that includes both benefits and tax effort. Second, even if they are used in conjunction with a benefit-effort index, unrestricted grants are not adequate unless the nation decides to equalize benefit-effort ratios at or above the level of the highest existing area. In all other cases, the Federal government must be able to tax state and local government tax collections. This is an essential policy instrument that no one has suggested creating.

For the perspective of an adequate Federal program, President Nixon's revenue-sharing proposals could be faulted on many counts.[8] (1) It has no provisions to insure minimum quantities of merit wants. (2) It has no provisions to handle the problems of externalities. (3) Its equalization formula is completely inadequate. Grants are to be distributed in accordance with an effort index, but not in accordance with a benefit-effort index. Thus, it concentrates aid on those communities with a taste for public goods, rather than on those communities that have low incomes. Since no tax on state and local tax collections is recommended, equalization could not occur even if the right benefit-effort index were used unless the Federal government were planning to contribute $35 billion to the equalization scheme. Such contributions are not contemplated.

A Further Complication

If each state and local government collected a set of taxes that was equivalent to a proportional tax on personal income, a system of grants-in-aid built out of the three components outlined above would be adequate to achieve society's goals. If state and local taxes are not proportional, but regressive or progressive, the Federal government could not achieve vertical equity (the optimum distribution of income) by simply placing its tax system on top of state and local tax systems. Differences in proportional tax rates from locality to locality can be handled in the system of grants-in-aid, but differences in the vertical structure of taxes cannot. The Federal government would need a different tax system for each state and locality. Federal taxes would have to be tailored to modify the locality's progressivity or regressivity so that the national desired distribution of income emerged.

The only other options are to insist that states and localities collect a set of taxes that are equivalent to proportional income taxes or to federalize state and local revenue collection. In reality, the first option would mean insisting that each state only collect taxes on personal income since our knowledge of incidence is not adequate to state the "personal income equivalence" of other taxes. The answer would probably have to be federalization of revenue collection.

In federalization, the Federal government would set its own tax rates to cover its own expenses and what it regards as an adequate level of state and local expenditures. The latter sum is simply turned back to states and localities in the form of the grant-in-aid formula outlined above. Equalization would involve only grants based on society's desired expenditure levels (there is no local revenue to tax). If state and local governments wish to exceed the general Federal expenditure standards, they would simply add a surtax to the Federal tax payments of individuals, or businesses located in their areas. The revenue from this surtax plus the other grant-in-aid payments would be turned over to the state or local government. If equalization of potential public incomes were desired, revenue yields would be based on average national per capita resources rather than upon the region's own revenues. Thus each man's Federal tax form would have four components. A set of rates that provided necessary Federal revenues, a surtax that provided a general level of revenue for state and local expenditures, a surtax that provided extra revenue for state governments if they so desired, and a surtax that provided extra revenue for local governments if they so desired. If states and localities did not want to reach the general Federal expenditure standards, they could add a negative surtax for the individuals in their areas, but they would still receive other grants-in-aid in accordance with the three-pronged grant-in-aid formula. They would simply make payments to the Federal government out of the unrestricted portion of their grants-in-aid.

Conclusions

To some extent the alteration in the distributions of economic resources produced by variations in state and local taxes are merely desirable expressions of different tastes for public goods in different areas. Were they merely to represent differences in tastes, the range of local tax structures would not be a defect of the American tax structure. Analysis indicates, however, that the present systems of integrating Federal, state, and local governments — earmarked grants-in-aid — is not adequate for handling the problems of externalities, merit wants, and vertical or horizontal equity created in a Federal tax structure. Substantial problems and inequities exist.

Analysis indicates that all of these problems are important enough to need correction, yet the proposed systems of unrestricted grants-in-aid will not solve the observed problems and inequities. These problems require structures of tax integration that are now far outside of the realm of political discussions.

Notes

1. *See* George F. Break, *Intergovernmental Fiscal Relations in the United States* (Washington, D.C.: The Brookings Institution, 1966), pp. 62–165, for a discussion of different grant schemes.
2. *See* L. Johansen, *Public Economics* (Chicago: Rand-McNally, 1965), pp. 9–22, for a demonstration of the relationships between policy targets and policy instruments. For an application to grant-in-aid, *see* Lester C. Thurow, "The Theory of Grants-in-Aid," *National Tax Journal* (December 1966), p. 373.
3. *See* Richard A. Musgrave, *The Theory of Public Finance* (New York: McGraw-Hill Book Co., 1959), pp. 13–14, for a discussion of merit grants.
4. Bureau of the Census, *Compendium of Public Employment, Census of Governments, 1962* (Washington, D.C.: Government Printing Office, 1963), p. 83. Expenditures are inflated or deflated by the ratio of each state's salaries to the national average.
5. This calculation assumes that the 1966–67 *state* benefit-effort ratios can be added to the 1962 local benefit-effort ratios. Thus, it is implicitly assuming that these ratios have not changed over the period.
6. *See* Lester C. Thurow, "A Fiscal Policy Model of the United States," *Survey of Current Business* (June 1969) (Washington, D.C.: Government Printing Office), pp. 53, 58, 62, for estimates of response elasticities.
7. This calculation assumes that the expenditure elasticity with respect to benefit-effort ratios is 1.
8. For a description of the Nixon proposals *see The Congressional Quarterly* (August 15, 1969), p. 1525 (September 5, 1969), p. 1646.

7 The Need for Wealth Taxes

Since the tax incidence analysis of Chapter 5 found that existing tax structure was regressive with respect to physical wealth, and since wealth taxes might be used to avoid the large excess burdens of income taxes, the whole structure of wealth taxation needs to be carefully examined. As wealth taxes have been virtually ignored in the modern literature on taxation, this chapter must analyze the existing structure of wealth taxes, the feasibility of a comprehensive wealth tax, and its possible economic effects. Before this can be done, however, it is necessary to analyze the appropriate role of wealth taxes in an overall structure of taxes.

When ideal systems of taxation are under discussion, income taxes and consumption taxes each have their proponents, but wealth taxes have generally been ignored.[1] Income taxes also are not viewed as an indirect instrument for taxing wealth. They are viewed as a tax upon income or as a tax upon potential consumption. Society presumably wants to achieve some distribution of income and is unconcerned about the distribution of wealth. In the literature on taxation the effects of wealth taxes, such as the property tax, are examined, but there is a general presumption that an ideal system of taxes would consist exclusively of either income or consumption taxes. Based on the analysis in this chapter, this view is incorrect. Wealth taxation is a central component in any ideal system of taxation.

The Appropriate Tax Base

As Chapter 4 indicated, there are a variety of distributions that might be examined to measure the impact of taxes. At the beginning of each year, an individual starts with some initial stock of economic goods or wealth (W_0). At the end of the year each individual has some final stock of wealth (W_1) and has consumed some quantity of goods and services (C_1). The individual's income during the year is simply the summation of his consumption activities and the net change in his wealth ($W_1 - W_0 + C_1 = Y_1$). Additions to wealth are identically equal to the individual's savings or dissavings ($S_1 = W_1 - W_0$). Thus income is equal to consumption plus savings ($Y_1 = C_1 + S_1$).

Within this accounting framework there are a variety of bases that might be taxed—wealth, consumption, and savings (additions to wealth). If income is chosen as the tax base, taxes are levied on consumption, plus additions to wealth. At no place in the framework, however, is there any basis for the distinction between realized and unrealized economic gains. Whether a person trades real assets for cash during the course of the year (realizes his gain) has no impact on wealth, consumption, or savings. Realization may affect the ease with which an individual can raise the necessary cash to pay his tax bills and the ease with which the tax collector can measure his economic positions, but it in no way affects his economic position or his economic ability to pay his tax bill. The necessity to raise cash to pay tax bills affects an individual's optimum portfolio balance and the desired degree of liquidity, but it does not affect his basic economic position.

The appropriate tax base or bases depend upon an analysis of the different types of benefits that flow from economic activity. These benefits fall essentially into two broad categories. Individuals receive economic benefits from (1) consuming economic goods and from (2) their power to control economic resources. Consumption is a measure of how much an individual takes out of the economic system. Wealth is a measure of an individual's potential power to control the use of economic resources.

Wealth, however, is composed of two major components—human capital (W^h) and physical capital (W^p). In an economy where each factor of production is paid its marginal product and where human and physical assets earn exactly the same rate of return for each individual (as they would in a perfect market), income is a perfect measure of each person's wealth. Each man's wealth is easily calculated by capitalizing his current and future income at the common rate of return on investment. Consequently, if society regards human and physical capital as indistinguishable and wishes to achieve some desired distribution of wealth (human plus physical), income is an appropriate tax base. Wealth and capitalized income are identical. Any desired distribution of total wealth can be obtained with some tax on income since the tax will itself be capitalized in determining the private value of wealth. Any given capital asset (human or physical) will thus have a different private value depending upon the tax bracket of the owner.

In any case, there are three major distributions that society may be interested in examining—the distribution of consumption, the distribution of human capital, and the distribution of physical wealth. The choice among these depends upon the theoretical underpinnings of the tax base.

If individual preferences are used to determine the appropriate proper tax base, economic resource should be measured as the simple summation of consumption expenditures, human wealth, and physical wealth. Economic man adjusts his consumption and savings decisions so that the marginal benefits from savings are equal to the marginal benefits from consumption. Since savings represent changes in wealth, the marginal benefits from wealth and consumption are brought into equilibrium. Being a rational investor he also equalizes the marginal benefits from human capital and physical capital. Thus the marginal benefits of consumption expenditures, human capital, and physical capital are equal for each person. As they are all equally beneficial, he should be taxed at some common rate on each. Therefore, the proper tax base is consumption plus wealth, and equity must be defined in terms of achieving the desired distributions of consumption plus wealth.

Several of the implications of this argument need to be realized. The correct tax base should be consumption plus wealth $(W_1 + C_1)$, not consumption plus increments to wealth $(W_1 - W_0 + C_1 = Y_1)$ as it is in an income tax. The total stock of wealth, not just increments to it, create economic benefits.

Alternatively, if an income tax is just an indirect wealth tax, the tax base should be consumption plus income $(C_1 + Y_1)$, but different tax rates must be levied on the two parts of the base since the goal is taxation of consumption plus wealth. For example, if the desired tax rate on consumption plus wealth is t, then t is the appropriate tax rate for consumption C_1, but the appropriate tax rate for income, Y_1, is t/r, where r is the common rate of return on wealth. Thus, if capital earns 10 percent per year, and a man's consumption tax rate is 20 percent, the appropriate tax rate for income is 200 percent $(0.20/0.10)$. If a man pays a 5 percent consumption tax, his appropriate income tax rate is 50 percent $(0.05/0.10)$.

Thus, if individual preferences are used to determine the appropriate tax base, the correct base is not income; it is consumption plus wealth. The individualistic approach, however, ignores society and its social-welfare function. While consumption, human wealth, and physical wealth may be equally valuable on the margin to an individual, they may not be equally valuable to society. Society may place different social-welfare values on different classes of economic resources just as it places different social-welfare values on the economic resources of different resource classes. It may have separate optimum distributions for each, or it may want to achieve some distribution where consumption, human wealth, and physical wealth are added together with different weights. If the social benefits per dollar of consumption were twice as large as the social benefits per dollar of human wealth, and four times as large as the social benefits per dollar of physical wealth, then capital should be taxed at twice the rate of consumption, and physical capital should be taxed at four times the rate of consumption. If the optimum distribution of wealth were wider than the optimum distribution of consumption, consumption tax rates would be much more progressive than wealth taxes. Thus, all the combinations or permutations among these bases may be possible depending upon society's social-welfare function (*see* Chapter 8). In any case, wealth should be one of the bases on which taxes are directly or indirectly levied. The only exception to this rule occurs when taxes bases are *not* based on individual preferences and when society is *not* concerned with the distribution of wealth in its social-welfare function.

Existing Physical Wealth Taxes

Although the United States has vestiges of wealth taxes, they are not generally viewed and justified as taxes designed to achieve society's desired distribution of wealth. They are usually regarded as historical anomalies that would be eliminated if optimum systems of either income or consumption taxes could be constructed. As was pointed out earlier, such is not the case. If we have physical wealth-distribution goals, a comprehensive wealth tax is necessary.

Historically the property tax was consciously designed as an instrument to tax wealth. Since all wealth was held in the form of land or buildings, the property tax could be used to control the distribution of wealth. The property tax still exists, but only 40 percent of net is now held in real estate, and since the importance of real estate differs from portfolio to portfolio, the property tax can be used neither to achieve the desired vertical distribution of wealth nor to achieve horizontal or rank-order equity.

The horizontal and rank-order inequities created by the property tax are often used as arguments against introducing a progressive rate structure to affect the vertical distribution of wealth. As the opponents point out, progression makes the horizontal and rank-order inequities greater in the upper ranges of net worth, but they neglect to mention that it reduces inequities in the lower net worth ranges. Whether the changes in the vertical distribution of wealth produced by a progressive rate structure are worth the increased inequality in upper ranges and the reduced inequality in lower ranges depends upon society's social-welfare function. In any case there is no way to use a tax that affects only 40 percent of total wealth to achieve the community's desired distribution of wealth and with the development of a modern economy, a tax that was once able to control the distribution of wealth has become inadequate.[2] Moreover, the property tax has an added disadvantage since it has been delegated to state and local governments. Even if all wealth were held in the form of real estate, the property tax could not be used to achieve society's desired distribution of wealth unless such decisions were centralized.

The estate and gift tax is also a tax on wealth, but it has several limitations as a device for achieving the desired distribution of wealth. The estate tax is a device that can be used to obtain society's desired intergenerational distribution of wealth, but it does not solve the problem of achieving the desired distribution of wealth at any one time. Society may wish to control the concentration of economic power in any one individual's hands over the course of his lifetime as well as control how much of this economic power he can transfer to his heirs.

At the moment, the estate and gift tax also is more of an illusion than a reality. Tax collections varied from 1.5 percent of income for those with incomes under $3,000 in 1965 to 5.3 percent of income for those with incomes over $15,000 with an average rate of 1.7 percent of total income.[3] Measured as a percent of total net worth, estate and gift taxes were levied at an average rate of 0.2 percent. Even if this tax were entirely levied on the group with net worth in excess of $500,000, it would still constitute a tax of less than 0.8 percent. Thus, as a practical matter, the estate and gift tax as it is presently constituted has little impact on individual incomes and almost no impact on the distribution of wealth.

The potential usefulness of the estate and gift tax depends upon the desired degree of equality in society's optimum distribution of wealth. The more infrequent the interval of taxation, the less equality the instrument is capable of achieving. With long intervals between tax collections, individuals have time to build up their wealth and to use their economic power. A once-in-a-lifetime wealth tax is capable of yielding less equality than a once-every-5-years wealth tax. The latter, in turn, can yield less equality than an annual wealth tax.

If society's desired distribution of wealth is not too equal, it can be achieved with wealth taxes at infrequent intervals. A severe tax could be levied once in each individual's lifetime (at death) or a lower tax could be levied at 1- or 5-year intervals. The choice depends upon other factors, such as the different impacts on saving, ease of collection, and the maximum amount of economic power an individual should be allowed to accumulate and exercise in his lifetime. Frequent wealth taxes can prevent *any* individual from accumulating too much economic power, while estate and gift taxes can only affect averages. Once in a lifetime taxes leave open the possibility that a few individuals will have enormous wealth, but it will be wealth that they accumulated, and not wealth that they inherited.

For the sake of illustration, assume that there is a 100 percent tax on inheritances and gifts in excess of $50,000. Since 93 percent of the households have less wealth than $50,000, and some of the wealth of those above this level comes from savings out of earnings, something less than 7 percent of the households would be affected by such a tax. If individuals received $50,000 at age zero and lived until age 70, consumed solely out of earned income, and received a 5 percent rate of return on investments, they would have $1.5 million at death. At age 35 they would have $275,800. If they received a 10 percent rate of return they would have $39.5 million at death, and $1.1 million at age 35. If they consumed half of their capital income, individuals with a 10 percent rate of return would leave $1.5 million at death, and individuals with a 5 percent rate of return would leave $281,500. If they could not receive $50,000 in gifts and inheritances until age 21 their wealth positions at death would be $\frac{1}{3}$ as great, with a 5 percent rate of return and $\frac{1}{8}$ as great with a 10 percent rate of return.

As these calculations indicate, even a very severe estate and gift tax would not place much of a potential constraint upon the maximum amount of wealth an individual could possess. Combined with savings out of earned income, individuals would still accumulate large fortunes.

Severe estate and gift taxes, however, would probably have a noticeable effect on the distribution of income. First, they would severely limit the number of individuals with wealth in the hundreds of millions. No one knows how many of these fortunes rest upon substantial initial inheritances, but many of them presumably fall into this category. Given the actual distribution of net worths and the almost complete absence of estate and gift taxes, it is also clear that many individuals must consume substantial proportions of their inheritance and its earnings, or they must receive low rates of return on their investments. If this were not the case, the distribution of wealth would be even more unequal than it is.

Currently, the 7.5 percent of the population with net worths in excess of $50,000 have 59.1 percent of total net worth, and the top 2.5 percent of the population with net worths in excess of $100,000 have 44 percent of total net worth.[4] The elderly are heavily represented among this latter group. Those over 65 years of age account for 37 percent of the wealth of the group with net worths in excess of $100,000. Inheritance taxes that prevented this wealth from being passed on to other wealthy individuals might substantially reduce the concentration of wealth.

Let us assume for the moment that existing patterns of inheritance are such that all of the wealth of the upper 2.5 percent of the population is either transferred to other individuals already in the upper 2.5 percent of the population, or is given in such large lumps that the receiver moves into the upper 2.5 percent (i.e., individual inheritances are at least $100,000 and on average are just as large as current average net worths among the top 2.5 percent). Moving to a system where no individual could inherit more than $50,000 from all sources would substantially alter the concentration of wealth under these circumstances. At age 65 life expectancy is 15 years and at a 5 percent rate of return 15 years are needed to bring a $50,000 inheritance up to $100,000.[5] In equilibrium there might be a net transfer of as much as 37 percent of the wealth held by those with wealth in excess of $100,000 to individuals with wealth of less than $100,000. This would reduce the proportion of total wealth held by the top 2.5 percent of the population by 16 percentage points—from 44 percent to 28 percent of total wealth.[6] If some of the wealth or income from it were consumed, the net reduction in the wealth of the top 2.5 percent of the population would be greater. Higher rates of return would lead to a smaller reduction. Thus a severe inheritance tax might have a substantial impact on the distribution of wealth.

At the same time, it is clear that a once-in-a-lifetime wealth tax is not a sensitive instrument for achieving society's desired distribution of wealth. It is too infrequent to place much of a constraint on an individual's wealth, although it might be an effective instrument for affecting the general shape of the wealth distribution. The choice between an effective estate and gift tax and a more frequent wealth tax comes down to a choice between whether society just wants to affect the general shape of the wealth distribution, or whether it wants to prevent individuals from having massive net worths and the economic power that goes with large fortunes. In the former case, an inheritance tax is a good instrument; in the latter case, a more frequent wealth tax must be used.

Feasibility

Before investigating a system of wealth taxes, however, a practical objection needs to be overcome. Often wealth taxes are cursorily dismissed on the grounds that the assessment problems are insurmountable. Many items that contributed to wealth have no easily accessible price since they are not frequently sold in the market place. Although the difficult practical problems should not be minimized, they should be put into perspective. Most wealth is in a form that is easily assessed or a form that society needs to assess for property taxes anyway.[7]

Householders' own homes account for 26.5 percent of total net worth, and their investments in property account for another 11.2 percent of net worth. In addition some unknown fraction of the net worth of privately owned businesses and professions represents the value of property. Since farms are included in this category, the fraction could be a substantial part (based on property assessments it might be as high as 50 percent) of the 17.3 percent of total net worth that is held in businesses or professions. No one denies that infrequently sold real estate is difficult to assess, but even now it must be assessed for the property tax. Assessing real estate for a wealth tax is no net burden on tax administration. In reality, the problems of frequent accurate property assessments are political and not economic.

Automobiles represent 2.8 percent of net worth, but their assessment does not present a problem, since they are a frequently sold commodity. Prices are easily available. The same situation exists with respect to stocks, 18.0 percent of net worth; marketable bonds, 2.0 percent of net worth; and liquid assets, 11.4 percent of net worth. The value of life insurance, annuities, and retirement plans, 6.1 percent of net worth, are not quite as easily available, but can easily be calculated. Personal debt, minus 2.1 percent of net worth, is also easy to assess.

The final category of assets used in this analysis is a miscellaneous category, 6.8 percent of net worth, which consists of assets held in trust; amounts that family members could have withdrawn from profit-sharing and other deferred income plans had they left their jobs; and such assets as oil royalties, patents, and commodity contracts. With the exception of patents, all of these items can rather easily be assessed.

This leaves some fraction of business and professional net worth as a difficult assessment item. It is doubtful whether such an assessment would be any harder than assessing real estate, but it would be a net burden on tax administration. It might also be possible to simply capitalize the businesses or professions income at some rate to determine the capitalized value of the business or profession, and to use averaging to eliminate short-run fluctuations. Such a procedure is not possible in real estate where individual homes are important, yet are not rented in the market, but it would be possible in the area of business and professional wealth.

Personal property, TV sets, furniture, jewels, paintings, etc. were left out of the Federal Reserve Board's calculations of net worth, but they do present an insurmountable problem if the focus is on evaluating every item of personal property. There is no need to do this, however. Many of these items are simply consumer's durables. Their distribution would be controlled with consumption taxes or income taxes. Other items of personal property, such as expensive jewels and paintings, are certainly part of personal wealth, but the assessment problem could be reduced to manageable proportions by trying to assess personal property of this type only when the total exceeded some figure such as $25,000. Individuals with personal property of this magnitude could easily be identified from insurance records.

Since there is no reason why a wealth tax should be collected annually, the magnitude of the assessment problem could be reduced by taxing each individual once every 5 years. Payments could be spread out over the succeeding 5 years to prevent individuals from having periodic liquidity problems. If the tax were applied at death, there would be no net increase in the burden on tax administration since such calculations are supposed to be made under current laws.

Reducing Excess Burdens

If wealth taxes exist by themselves or are not comprehensive, they are subject to all of the incidence, shifting, and excess burden problems endemic in a system of income taxes. When they are imposed, individuals invest less in their capital, human or physical, to hold the posttax rate of return at their rate of time preference. Savings fall; consumption increases. The result is less potential output and an excess burden.

Although wealth taxes cannot solve the excess burden problem, they can reduce it when used in conjunction with a system of consumption taxes to control the distribution of consumption. Shifting and excess burdens are created when it is possible to avoid or reduce taxes by undertaking different economic activities. If such tax reductions are not possible, the patterns of economic activity are not apt to change.

In theory it would be necessary to have a system of leisure taxes as well as wealth and consumption taxes to fully suppress excess burden, but our earlier analysis indicated that individuals do not avoid taxes by increasing their leisure and lowering their incomes. They do exactly the opposite. Thus an integrated set of wealth taxes and consumption taxes could eliminate the positive excess burdens of the present tax system without a set of leisure taxes.

Assume for the sake of discussion that the system of wealth taxes is composed of an earned income tax to control the distribution of human capital and a comprehensive tax on physical wealth. If the rate structures on human capital (earned income) and consumption are set more progressively than the rate structures on physical wealth, a utility-maximizing individual with consumption, human capital, and wealth as three equally weighted arguments in his utility function will find that moving into either human capital investment or consumption increases rather than reduces the total taxes that he must pay. Altering his investment pattern reduces his total utility below what it would be if he did not reduce his investment wealth. He will in fact have an incentive to shift out of consumption and human capital into physical capital since the rate structure is less progressive for physical capital. If consumption, human capital, and physical capital enter the individual's utility function in different ways, these conclusions do not necessarily hold, but individuals will, in general, shift into that commodity with the least progressive rate structure. In any case, shifting can be reduced by the proper structure of other taxes.

Since much of the investment in human capital is undertaken by governments and since there are substantial noneconomic benefits from education, the major excess burdens of taxation are created by reductions in the stock of physical capital. To prevent such reductions, consumption tax rates must be closely integrated with the tax rates on physical wealth. In essence consumption tax rates must be set so that they forestall any reduction in savings. This means a consumption tax schedule that is much more progressive than the tax schedule for physical wealth. But it should be emphasized that it does not necessarily mean high average consumption tax rates or a reliance on consumption taxes. (Technically, progressive consumption taxes are easy to collect in a tax system that is also collecting taxes on physical wealth and earned income.) Given that consumption tax rates can and should exceed 100 percent in the upper ranges of consumption, there is no doubt that a sufficiently progressive consumption tax can overwhelm any incentive to reduce savings that may be created by a wealth tax.

Conclusions

A comprehensive wealth tax is not only feasible, it is a necessary ingredient in an adequate system of taxation. This is true regardless of whether the theoretical basis of the tax system is individual preferences or social-welfare judgments. A comprehensive wealth tax would probably be split into an income tax on earned incomes as a means of indirectly taxing human capital and a direct tax on physical wealth. Within the category of physical wealth, all types of assets should be taxed at common rates, unless some of the assets benefit from special government services and should be subject to users' taxes.

Used in conjunction with an integrated set of consumption taxes, most of the current excess burdens of taxation could be avoided. Thus from both the perspective of potential benefits to be gained and the current costs to be eliminated, wealth taxes merit inclusion in any adequate system of taxes.

Notes

1. Henry C. Simons, *Personal Income Taxation* (Chicago: University of Chicago Press, 1930); Kaldor Nichols, *An Expenditure Tax* (London: Allen & Unwin, 1955).
2. Board of Governors of Federal Reserve System, "Survey of Financial Characteristics," *Federal Reserve Bulletin* (March 1964), p. 293.
3. *Tax Burdens and Benefits of Government Expenditures by Income Class, 1961 and 1965* (New York: Tax Foundation, 1967), p. 20.
4. *See* Table 8-4, Chapter 8.
5. Census Bureau, *Statistical Abstract 1969*, p. 54.
6. Calculated on the assumption that everyone dies by age 75.
7. Distribution of wealth across different asset types is taken from *Federal Reserve Bulletin* (March 1964).

8 Political Judgments and Economic Welfare

Since taxes are ultimately levied to improve economic welfare, society must determine how various distributions of economic resources contribute to promoting economic welfare. Only then can it set its tax structure in such a manner as to obtain the most welfare. This process of setting taxes, however, requires some operational definition of when welfare is rising or falling.

Thus this chapter is concerned with distribution goals and with the related questions of individual preferences versus social preferences. It asks how the concept of equity can be defined and measured, and how it can aid taxation in its search to achieve an optimum distribution of economic resources.

Social Balance

The conditions that exist when the economy is in its optimum welfare position (social balance) are easy to define. The problem is in determining where these conditions exist and whether the economy is getting closer to them. To bring the economy into "social balance" the social rate of return on private investment projects and the social rate of return on public investment projects must be equal to the social rate of time preference (the rate at which society is willing to trade future consumption goods for current consumption goods); and the marginal social welfare of private consumption expenditures must be equal to the marginal social welfare of public consumption expenditures.[1] In addition the distribution of resources among private individuals is to be such that each individual has the same marginal social welfare (*see below*).

To achieve social balance in a market economy taxes must perform two roles. They must transfer enough resources from the private sector to the public sector to equalize the marginal social rates of return on private and public consumption and on private and public investment. And they must transfer resources among private individuals in such a manner as to equalize the marginal social welfare of each individual.

Although taxes are necessary to achieve social balance in a market economy, they also make its achievement impossible. Individual investment decisions are based upon after-tax rates of return on investment projects; yet the social returns on these same investments include tax payments since tax payments represent resources that the community can use. If the social rate of time preference is a weighted average of individual rates of time preference, private investments, on average, will be made until the after-tax rate of return on investment equals the social rate of time preference.[2] Thus, the social rate of return (the pretax rate of return) will be greater than the rate of time preference. From society's standpoint there will be too little private investment.[3]

The problem occurs in all tax systems except a lump-sum tax system but such a system cannot meet redistribution goals. Eliminating the income tax merely moves the problem from one area to another. If consumption taxes were substituted for income taxes, consumers would purchase public and private consumption goods until their marginal utilities are equal, but private consumption expenditures now would include some tax payments. As a result, the price of private consumption expenditures rises, and the marginal utility per dollar of private consumption expenditures falls. To bring utilities back into equilibrium, private consumption expenditures are cut back, and public consumption expenditures are expanded. The result is to once again move the economy away from its position of social balance.

Since private investors quit investing before the social rate of return equals the social rate of time preference, there is no method for bringing the social rate of return on private investments into line with the social rate of time preference. The social rate of return on public investments can be brought into equilibrium with the social rate of return on private investments by reducing public investment, but equalization just means that both public and private investments are too small.

Thus economies with private sectors are forced to choose between equalizing the rate of return on public investment projects and the social rate of time preference or equalizing the rate of return on public and private investment projects. In the first case the private rate of return on investment projects is higher than the social rate of time preference, and in the second case both the private and public rates of return on investment projects are too high.

Using partial equilibrium analysis the first case is to be preferred to the second since one rather than two of the conditions of social balance are violated. As a result most decision rules for public investment opt for equalizing the social rate of return on public investment with the social rate of time preference. For example, in opportunity-cost approaches to public investment decisions, efforts are made to determine the opportunity costs of funds to taxpayers (social discount rate). Given opportunity costs, public investments are made until the rate of return on investment projects reaches the level determined by taxpayer's opportunity costs.

Using general equilibrium analysis and the theory of the second best, the same simple conclusions cannot be reached. In general, it is not possible to say that violating one condition of social balance is better than violating two conditions of social balance. In each case an empirical analysis would have to be made showing the changes caused by violating one or two conditions. The welfare implications of these changes would then be evaluated using society's social-welfare function.

No set of taxes can solve this dilemma. All taxes keep the economy from obtaining social balance at some point. Practically the problem cannot be eliminated. Taxes are necessary instruments to achieve social balance in a market economy; yet they also make the achievement of social balance impossible. The economy may be closer to social balance with taxes than without taxes, but it can never achieve social balance as long as some investment decisions are made privately.

The Market Distribution of Private Resources

Taxes need go beyond merely increasing the resources of the public sector since market economies do not automatically generate distributions of resources that yield an equalization of individual marginal social welfares. This is important since the distribution of economic resources plays a central role in the allocation of goods and services. Individual preferences determine market demands, but preferences are weighted by economic resources before they are communicated to the market. If an individual has no resources, his potential demand for goods and services has no effect on the market. He must have resources with which to make his preferences felt.

The efficiency of a market system depends on the prior achievement of an optimum distribution of economic resources. If income is distributed in accordance with society's preferences, individual preferences are properly weighted in the marketplace, and the market can then efficiently adjust to an equitable set of demands. If income is not distributed in accordance with the community's preferences, the market adjusts to an inequitable set of demands. Market signals do not express society's desires and the market system does not result in an acceptable distribution of goods and services.

Although a market system may efficiently handle the demands for goods and services flowing from a community's desired distribution of economic resources, there is nothing in a market system that automatically generates or regenerates the desired distributions. One of the major continuing functions of government in a market economy is thus to insure that the market is responding to the desired distribution of economic resources.

Since one of the major functions of taxes is to create an optimum distribution of private resources, each society must explicitly or implicitly choose a desired distribution of economic resources or ratify the distribution that is produced in the market. Without such a desired distribution it is impossible to levy taxes.

Moreover, each society's desired distribution of economic resources will depend upon its definition of equity. It must decide what distributions are equitable and what distributions are inequitable.

Before we proceed to the concept of equity, the limited circumference of economics should be clearly marked out. Tax collections are not designed to achieve equity in the broadest senses of that term. Only *economic* equity is really under consideration. Noneconomic goods — health, friends, beauty, etc. — are not taxed, yet they can increase welfare, utility, or satisfaction just as much or more than economic goods. Each of these goods may be inequitably distributed. They are not taxed because it is impossible to design economic systems for taxing them, but this does not lessen their importance. Man's economic activities are not his highest art form; they are merely a set of activities that make higher art forms possible. The difficulties of measuring noneconomic goods means that they are not taxed, but it also means that the distribution of their benefits cannot be used to evaluate the taxes that an individual should pay on his economic goods. To be ultimately equitable the beautiful girl should have to pay higher tax rates on her income than the ugly girl, but how do you build this into a workable tax code?

In order to argue that a tax system that ignores noneconomic goods is equitable one of two strong assumptions must be made. (1) If every individual receives the same benefits from noneconomic goods so that all differences in welfare are produced by economic goods, economic taxes can be levied to achieve any desired distribution of welfare since they control the only factor that can lead to differences in total welfare. (2) If noneconomic goods are distributed in some fixed relation to economic goods, tax rates can be set to reflect the benefits of economic and noneconomic goods even though they can only be levied on economic goods. Since neither assumption is true, no system of economic taxes can be equitable from some larger welfare viewpoint. They can only be *economically equitable*.

In practice, actual tax systems do not even cover the entire set of economic goods. Only those economic goods that are bought and sold in the market are typically taxed. The benefit flowing from personal services, housewife's services, do-it-yourself, the backyard garden, and a host of other self-produced economic goods stand outside of the tax system. To justify this exclusion theoretically requires assumptions analogous to those outlined above. Every individual must receive the same benefit from self-produced economic goods, or every individual must receive benefits from self-produced economic goods in some fixed relation to his marketable economic goods. As with noneconomic goods, neither is true. In practice equity comes to mean an equitable distribution of *marketable economic* resources.

Optimum Distributions of Resources: The Concept of Equity

Classical Definitions. The concept of equity falls into two categories, vertical equity and horizontal equity. Their origins are lost in the long history of public finance,[4] but if the distinction was not made by the world's first tax collector, it was made soon thereafter. The two concepts, however, are not independent. Achieving vertical equity—proper disparity in economic resources between rich and poor—requires the achievement of horizontal equity—the equal treatment of equals. This can be seen by looking at the definitions of vertical equity.

Three concepts of vertical equity have been distinguished— *equal absolute sacrifice, equal proportional sacrifice,* and *equal marginal sacrifice.*[5] Taxes are to be levied so that total utility losses are equal for all individuals, so that each individual sacrifices the same proportion of his total utility, and so that the utility loss from the marginal tax dollar is equal for each individual. Regardless of the sacrifice principle, individuals with the same economic resources and the same utility schedules must be taxed equally in order to achieve vertical equity. Thus the achievement of vertical equity automatically creates horizontal equity, but what constitutes horizontal equity differs within each differing definition of vertical equity (*see below*).

The three previous definitions of vertical equity, and thus horizontal equity, have two fundamental drawbacks. First, they are not operational. Since utility functions are not known, and will not be revealed, there is no method to levy taxes in accordance with the principles of vertical and horizontal equity. Second, they ignore the existence of a social welfare function. More precisely, if taxes are collected in such a manner as to maximize social welfare or minimize the losses in social welfare from tax collections, each of the sacrific principles implies a particular social-welfare function.

If the social-welfare function is the simple unweighted summation of each individual utility function (*see* Equation 1), maximizing social welfare calls for taxing each individual so that the marginal utility losses from the marginal tax dollar are equal for all individuals. Thus horizontal equity is defined in terms of equal marginal losses. When each individual suffers the same marginal losses of utility there will be some after-tax distribution of utilities. This distribution is the definition of vertical equity. Conversely, equal marginal sacrifice will not maximize the social-welfare function unless it is the simple unweighted summation of each individual utility function.

Equal proportion sacrifice defines vertical equity in terms of a particular definition of horizontal equity. Every person is to suffer the same proportional loss in utility from taxation. The after-tax distribution of utilities constitutes the definition of vertical equity. Such a principle maximizes social welfare if the social-welfare function is the simple unweighted summation of individual utilities where each individual is assumed to have the same total amount of utility (*see* Equation 2). There are a variety of methods for standardizing utility functions so that each individual has the same total amount of utility, but the different methods are irrelevant here (in Equation 2 total utility has arbitrarily been set equal to 1 for each individual). With such a social-welfare function the way to minimize the social-welfare losses from taxes is to take the same proportional amount of utility away from each individual.

The equal absolute sacrifice principle also defines vertical equity in terms of horizontal equity, but it uses a different definition of horizontal equity. Every person is to suffer the same absolute loss in utility from taxation. Once again, the after-tax distribution of utilities constitutes the definition of vertical equity. Such a principle maximizes social welfare if the social-

welfare function is a simple unweighted summation of the
summation of the marginal utilities of economic resources for
each individual (*see* Equation 3). Each individual's total utility in
the social-welfare function is given by the marginal utility of his
first unit of economic resources plus the marginal utility of his
second unit of economic resources plus the marginal utility of
his third unit of economic resources, etc. Thus the measurement
of utility includes an "owner's surplus" that is comparable to the
"consumer's surplus." With this social-welfare function, taking
the same absolute amount of utility away from each individual is
the way to minimize the total social-welfare losses from taxes.

(1) $$SW = \sum_{i=1}^{n} U(E)_i$$

(2) $$SW = \sum_{i=1}^{n} \frac{U(E)_i}{U(E)_i}$$

(3) $$SW = \sum_{i=1}^{n} \left(\sum_{j=1}^{m} MU(E)_j \right)_i$$

where

SW = social welfare
n = number of individuals in society
E = economic resources
i = ith individual
$U(E)_i$ = total utility of economic resources of individual i
$[MU(E)_j]_i$ = marginal utility of jth unit of economic resources
for individual i
m_i = units of economic resources possessed by the ith
individual

Since social-welfare functions are the device through which
the community evaluates, compares, and weighs the positions of
different individuals, the first and third social welfare functions
are peculiar. Individuals get to determine their own weight in
the social-welfare function. If they place a high marginal utility
on economic resources they are taxed less than those who place
a low marginal utility on economic resources. The rich miser is
taxed less than the poor man who does not worry about economic
resources. Individual utility functions are just added together to

create a social-welfare function. Thus in some sense society evades its responsibilities since it does not use its social-welfare function to evaluate, compare, and weigh different individuals.

In the second social-welfare function, society does not evade this responsibility. It weighs the utility of each individual, but there is no particular justification for the chosen weights. Does the community really want to assume that each person has the same total utility or level of enjoyment regardless of the economic resources that he controls? Unless the community wants to make this assumption, equal proportional sacrifice cannot be justified as a principle of taxation.

Society must make similar specific choices to justify either equal marginal sacrifice or equal absolute sacrifice. Does the community really want an additive social-welfare function with individual utilities as the arguments? Why not choose a multiplicative function or one where weights are attached to different amounts of economic resources or to different individuals? Unless the community wants an additive unweighted function, equal marginal sacrifice cannot be justified. Equal absolute sacrifice requires a peculiar social-welfare function where society chooses to evaluate all units of economic resources at their marginal value. Why should it want to do so? In economics all units of economic resources are normally evaluated at the value of the marginal unit, but here the "owners' surplus" is taken into account. Why shift the evaluation procedure? Unless the evaluation procedure is shifted, equal absolute sacrifice cannot be justified.

On a more fundamental level, it is questionable whether individual utility functions should appear as the arguments in the social welfare function. Normally such a procedure is justified as a method for taking individual preferences into account in social welfare decisions. Using utility functions as the arguments of the social-welfare function, however, is the wrong method of achieving this end. Individual preferences should determine the form of the social welfare function and the nature of its arguments, but they should not allow each individual to determine his own importance in the social welfare function. When utility functions appear in the social welfare function, this is exactly what is happening. The real problem is finding a decision rule for *constructing* social welfare functions that can take individual preferences into account in a sensible way.[6] None of the three neoclassical sacrifice principles seem to be a particular plausible answer to this problem.

An appropriate welfare function must be found, however, to judge the impact of taxes on the distribution of economic resources. For example, using the equal marginal sacrifice principle the correct point of reference is the individual taxpayer. To determine the welfare incidence of taxes it is necessary to know how taxes are levied, how these taxes affect the distribution of economic resources, and the utility function for each individual taxpayer. Both the shape and the arguments (those factors that produce utility—income, consumption, leisure, wealth, etc.) must be known for each individual. Given these pieces of information, tax incidence is measured by subtracting vectors of individual utilities with and without taxes and expenditures or with and without taxes of different types. This type of incidence might be called "personal" incidence.

As McGuire and Aaron demonstrate, the personal incidence of taxes differs depending on the nature of individual utility functions.[7] This is true regardless of whether each individual has the same utility function or different utility functions. (McGuire and Aaron assume each individual has the same utility function.) Thus an individual with many resources and with high marginal utility of resources may have a high "personal" incidence of taxes even if taxes did not substantially reduce his economic resources.

Defining tax incidence in terms of personal incidence presents several problems. First, it is impossible to know, either theoretically or empirically, individual utility functions. Individuals simply will not reveal them to a tax collector if they know that this information is going to be used in tax assessment. Theoretically postulated utility functions, such as those used by McGuire and Aaron, have no particular validity.

Second, when the individual perspective is being used it is not possible to limit the analysis to economic resources. Utility is produced by a host of noneconomic conditions. These conditions must be known and evaluated when constructing the vectors of utility that are to be compared. No one can judge whether the tax system is creating the right distribution of utilities if he only looks at the utility produced by economic resources. It is even impossible. Unless the individual's position on his utility function is known, it is impossible to calculate the marginal utility of economic goods, yet an individual's position on his utility function cannot be known without knowing all of his economic and noneconomic conditions.

Third, as previously mentioned the individual perspective is valid only if each individual is to be allowed to determine his own weight in the social-welfare function. In a democracy individual preferences should be used in formulating the decision rules for constructing a social-welfare function, but there is no reason why social welfare should be a function of individual utilities.

If, on the other hand, the social-welfare function is used to compare and evaluate individuals, it must be known in order to judge welfare effects. From this point of view vectors of social welfare are constructed that list the social welfare ascribed to each individual with and without taxes and expenditures or with and without taxes of different types. Subtracting vectors of social welfare provides the measure of incidence—a measure that might be called "social" incidence.

For the purposes of levying taxes social incidence rather than personal incidence is desired. Society levies taxes to obtain the community's desired distribution of social welfare, not the individual's desired utility level. There are two broad avenues for constructing vectors of social welfare. The community may decide to let individual utilities enter the social-welfare function, but weight individual utilities with socially determined weights. Or it may decide to ascribe social-welfare values directly to different amounts of economic resources. As a practical matter, the latter is the only feasible alternative. There is no method for constructing a measure of social welfare based upon unknowable utilities. In addition, society seems to subscribe verbally to the principle that individuals with the same economic resources should pay the same taxes. Perhaps horizontal equity is defined in terms of economic resources because there is no other practical method, but more fundamental reasons seem to lie behind such a definition. The community does not seem to believe that individual variations in the utility generated by identical economic resources should be given weight in the tax structure.

Operational Definitions of Equity. If social-welfare values are then to be ascribed directly to different levels of economic resources, it is first necessary to know the actual distribution of economic resources. This is why Chapter 4 calculates such distributions. Economists cannot construct distributions of social welfare because they cannot estimate social welfare any more than they can estimate personal utilities. The ultimate social welfare judgments must come from the political process. The economist can only calculate the distribution of economic resources with and without taxes and expenditure or with and without taxes of different types. The political process must translate them into distributions of social welfare.

The community must directly decide how much of its total resources should go to different groups of individuals. Should the wealthiest 10 percent of the population have 50 percent of total income, 25 percent, or 10 percent? Should the poorest 10 percent of the population have 1 percent of total income, 5 percent, or 10 percent? How large a gap should be allowed between the richest and poorest citizens? How closely should the distribution of income be concentrated around the median income? These are the essential questions that a society must ask when it sets its tax policies. Until these basic decisions have been made, tax and other economic policies cannot be designed to achieve society's goal of vertical equity, but the answers to these questions are not to be found within economics. They lie within the province of moral philosophy.

Depending upon society's desires, any distribution of income could be an equitable distribution of income. Explicitly or implicitly, however, every society has some definition of vertical equity. Either it explicitly sets out its optimum distribution of resources, or it implicitly accepts whatever resources distribution is produced by the market place and its tax laws. In either case, it has a standard of vertical equity.

In a democracy, social decisions concerning the optimum distribution of resources presumably spring from three factors.
First, individuals and society may simply have a taste for equality
or inequality, just as they have a taste for paintings. We may like
to live in a society which more or less equally distributes resources.[8] Second, the distribution of resources may produce
externalities. Strong inequalities may produce crime, social
unrest, political unrest, and a host of other ailments. If such is
the case (and there is a general presumption to this effect),
society may want to limit dispersions to avoid unpleasant
consequences. Third, individual utility functions may contain
the resources of other individuals as one of their arguments.[9] If
my welfare increases when my neighbour's income increases, I
may vote to redistribute some of my income to maximize my
own welfare.

As a country grows richer the optimum resource distribution
may become more or less disperse. An argument can be made
that equality is desirable in a poor country where everyone is
close to subsistence. Small inequalities might push someone
below the subsistence line. In a richer country, the consequences
of inequalities are not so important. In this view, equality is an
inferior good. The richer we become, the less of it we need.

A contrary argument is based on economic growth. Maximizing economic output may be so important in a poor country
that society is willing to tolerate inequalities among individuals
if this is necessary to produce rapid growth. Since an equal
sharing of the existing output might result in misery for everyone without the prospect of future growth, a decision is made to
share misery unequally in the hopes of eliminating future
misery.[10] Here it is assumed that an unequal distribution of
output will lead to more savings, more investments, and a higher
growth rate. A conscious decision is made that individuals who
are living today should have unequal incomes so that all individuals in the future may have a higher standard of living. As
output increases, however, the value attached to increases in
output for future generations probably decreases. Future man
will be relatively rich in comparison with present man; neither
are in misery on average. Consequently, the benefits attached to
future growth produced by inequalities gradually diminish.

Thus, the relative importance of achieving a more equal distribution of output rises as average output levels rise, even if there is no shift in preferences about the benefits of achieving a more equal income distribution. From this vantage point, equality is a superior good. The richer we become, the more of it we can afford.

There is also no reason why our social-welfare function and our equity decisions cannot change over time. Our tastes concerning the desired income distribution may simply change. In recent centuries Western societies seem to have moved in the direction of more equality.

While it is impossible to avoid implicitly choosing some standard of vertical equity, it is not necessary to subscribe to any standard of horizontal equity. If tax rates were distributed according to a giant lottery within each income class, it would be possible to reach society's desired income distribution—vertical equity—without achieving horizontal equtiy—the equal treatment of equals. Although most societies verbally subscribe to the principle of horizontal equity, there is no logical necessity that they must do so. The failure of a tax system to achieve horizontal equity does not mean that it has failed to achieve its equity goals unless horizontal equity, however defined, is one of the goals.

In addition to vertical and horizontal equity, there is a third equity principle that most societies endorse. This principle is often included in horizontal equity, but it does not logically flow from that concept. It might be called the goal of rank-order equity. Rank-order equity means that the tax system should not alter the rank order of incomes produced in the market place. The differences in welfare between the wealthiest man pretax and the poorest man pretax may be reduced or eliminated, but the poorest man pretax is not left wealthier posttax than the wealthiest man posttax (everything else being the same). Both the desired distribution of income and the equal taxation of equal incomes can be achieved without achieving rank-order equity. The reverse is also true. Rank-order equity can be achieved without achieving vertical equity, but it does imply horizontal equity.

Thus taxes can be judged with respect to any of these three equity goals, but they all require some form of political definition.

Social Welfare and the Appropriate Tax Base

Given that distributions of economic resources appear directly in the social-welfare function, there is a problem of determining the appropriate tax base. Consumption plus wealth, the appropriate base from the individualistic perspective, may or may not be the appropriate tax base from the perspective of society. Society may wish to achieve different distributions of consumption and wealth rather than some common distribution. But why should this be so? The answer goes back to externalities and tastes. As a society, we may simply have different tastes concerning the distribution of consumption privileges and the distribution of different types of economic power. Thus we might decide that consumption privileges should be equally distributed (implying a tax system with some level of personal exemptions coupled with an infinite tax rate on additional consumption expenditures), that each person should have some minimum quantity of human capital (implying a tax system with a per capita grant—negative tax), and that no individual should have market economic power over another individual due to his physical wealth (implying a 100 percent tax rate on physical wealth). From the point of view of social tastes, no set of preferences about the desired or optimum distribution of consumption, human wealth, or physical wealth implies anything about the desired optimum distribution of the others. Society must choose its three optimum distributions or its desired common distributions.

Externalities are important because different sets of externalities may be associated with the distributions of consumption, human wealth, and physical wealth. Crime, social unrest, political unrest, and other factors may be differentially affected by the three distributions. If they are, the distribution of consumption that is optimum with respect to externalities (positive or negative) may be different from the distribution of human wealth or physical wealth. This is apt to be the case, since there are sharp distinctions between consumption privileges, the economic power that is embedded in human capital, and the economic power associated with physical capital. The distribution of consumption affects living standards and the sense of enjoyment or deprivation that they receive from these living standards. It affects a man's position in his role as a consumer. The distribution of human capital primarily affects the individual in his role as a producer. It influences the types of work he will be able to do and the personal benefits he will receive from being a productive citizen. Human capital may also create technical progress that cannot be captured by the individual who actually makes the innovation. It may be necessary to preserve self-esteem in a working society.

The distribution of physical wealth, on the other hand, affects man in his role as a producer, but in a different manner. Physical wealth allows an individual to direct the productive activities of other individuals. Since physical wealth is salable, while human wealth is not, physical wealth can be turned into political power (through campaign contributions) more easily than human wealth. Thus the distribution of physical wealth may have a large impact on the distribution of political power. If we want a relatively equal distribution of political power, we may have to have a relatively equal distribution of physical wealth.

The community might also decide that individual decisions lead to too much consumption and too little investment. In making such a decision society decides that the social welfare value of consumption and savings are not equal for the community although they might be equal for each individual. In this case, there is no reason why the tax base should not reflect the difference between social perspectives and individual perspectives on consumption-savings decisions.

If society wishes to achieve separate optimum distributions of consumption, human wealth, and physical wealth, or if it wishes to achieve some weighted average of these three, there must be at least three different taxes or the government must be pursuing some of these objectives via other policy instruments (transfer payments and subsidies are considered negative taxes). If expenditure instruments are not being used, there is no method for achieving all three optimum distributions or a weighted distribution with less than three taxes. Taxes may affect more than one of the distributions, but the effects must be modified with other taxes that allow society to reach its separate optimum distributions. For example, if society has different distributional goals for human capital and physical capital, the income tax can be used as one of the necessary tax instruments, but a specific human capital or physical capital tax must be used with it. Essentially, the income tax would be set to yield the desired distribution of either human capital or physical capital, and the other tax would be placed on top of it in such a way as to yield the other desired distribution. The need for tax instruments beyond the income tax is equally urgent when society desires the same but separate distributions of consumption, human capital, and physical capital. The income tax can be used to control the distribution of human wealth plus physical wealth, but it cannot be used to establish two separate distributions of human wealth and physical wealth. It cannot in any sense be used to control consumption in a world in which individuals have wealth that can be turned into consumption. Thus the income tax is an adequate instrument only when society wishes to achieve some distribution of human wealth plus physical wealth and is not interested in consumption expenditures.

Keeping the separate goals of distributing consumption, human capital, and physical capital clearly in mind helps eliminate many of the arguments that occur as to whether this or that should be included in some tax. Take the question of the appropriate tax rate for capital gains. Should they be taxed at the same rate as income, or at some other rate? If the capital gains are spent on consumption, they should be taxed at the rate appropriate to consumption. If capital gains are not spent, but added to capital, they should be taxed at the rates appropriate to wealth. If society has an optimum distribution of human plus physical wealth, capital gains should be taxed at the same rate as income since this is the only way that wealth can be fairly taxed. If society has different optimum tax rates for human capital and for physical capital, capital gains on physical capital should be taxed at the rate applied to physical capital generally. Taxing capital gains fairly does not, however, involve arguing about whether increases in the value of old wealth are equivalent to additions to new wealth (savings). The value of wealth is to be taxed. How the value materialized (through changing prices or savings) is irrelevant.

Conclusions

Although the conditions that an optimum tax structure is supposed to create are easily defined, political value judgments are necessary to say whether these conditions do or do not exist. Economics cannot provide the answer. Economics can only determine the actions that would be necessary to achieve social balance once it has been operationally defined.

Although the political process should be making the necessary value judgments, it does so only by default. As a society we have not properly debated the shapes that our distributions of resources should assume. Given this lack of discussion, it is impossible to determine whether the existing tax structure promotes or demotes economic welfare.

Notes

1. For a discussion of social balance *see* Bernard P. Herber, *Modern Public Finance, 1967* (Homewood, Ill.: Richard D. Irwin, 1967), chaps. 1–4.
2. If the social rate of time preference is not derived from a weighted average of individual rates of time preference. There is no necessary connection between the social rate and individual rates of time preference. After-tax rates of return would equal the social rate of time preference only by accident.
3. For a discussion of this problem *see* W. J. Baumol, "On the Social Discount Rate," *American Economic Review* (September 1968), p. 788.
4. In recent history the distribution has been associated with Henry C. Simons, *Personal Income Taxation* (Chicago: University of Chicago Press, 1938), chap. 1.
5. For a discussion of the different sacrifice principles *see* Richard A. Musgrave, *The Theory of Public Finance* (New York: McGraw-Hill Book Co., 1959), p. 96.
6. For a discussion of the problems of doing this *see* Kenneth J. Arrow, *Social Choice and Individual Values* (New York: John Wiley & Sons, 1959).
7. From an investigation of how individual utility functions affect personal tax incidence *see* Henry Aaron and Martin C. McGuire, "Benefits and Burdens of Government Expenditures," *Econometrica* (forthcoming).
8. For a discussion of the income distribution's public good characteristics *see* Lester C. Thurow, "The Income Distribution as a Pure Public Good," *Quarterly Journal of Economics* (May, 1971).
9. For some of the implications of this motive for redistribution *see* Harold M. Hochman and James D. Rodgers, "Pareto Optimal Redistribution," *American Economic Review* (September 1969), p. 542.
10. This problem can be avoided by treating everyone equitably and saving publically, but many governments find it difficult to save for industrial projects.

9 Priorities for a Tax Policy

To draw conclusions from the previous analysis it is necessary to go beyond what can be logically deduced from the first principles of economics or from any other set of noncontroversial assumptions. Value judgments must be inserted into the analysis if public policy recommendations are to be made. The conclusions in this chapter are based on the value judgments that I perceived to be those of a majority of the American public. They are not my value judgments since I would opt for more equality than is implicit in the value judgments used here, but I may be misreading the opinions of my fellow citizens. In any case the judgments are made explicit, and the implications of some alternatives will be discussed.

The Political Process

To specify appropriate tax bases or rates, a country must determine the shape and arguments of its social-welfare function. What factors are in the social-welfare function and how do they contribute to economic welfare? Since the classical sacrifice principles (*see* Chapter 8) have no particular validity and are unusable in any case, there are no principles in welfare economics or the economics of taxation that allow a community to deduce its social-welfare function. Some alternative technique must be found. In a democracy and holding the belief that individual preferences should be used in constructing the community's social-welfare function, the only alternative is to construct the social-welfare function in the political arena.

This places a burden on the political arena. If individual citizens are to be able to make informed judgments, debates on social welfare priorities should be conducted openly and explicitly so the average citizen can know what is happening. If some group of individuals is getting favorable treatment in either taxes or expenditures, the rest of society should know this so that they can agree or disagree with the preferences. Unless this happens individual preferences cannot possibly be used in constructing the community's social-welfare function.

On such a criterion, the American political system receives low marks in the area of taxation. Instead of making social value judgments clear and explicit, deliberate efforts are made to hide special privileges. The result is the enormous difference between nominal and effective rates in the Federal personal income tax (*see* Chapter 1). The only possible purpose of such a gap is to trick the American public into thinking that its preferences for a progressive income tax are being implemented when they are not. The same phenomenon can be seen in the Census Bureau's failure to collect data on the distribution of wealth. Technical difficulties are always cited, but such difficulties are no more prevalent in wealth collection than in many other areas from which data are collected. Without such data it is impossible for the public to know whether it does or does not need wealth taxes or what the appropriate rate structure should be. The political platforms of the major political parties are also remarkably silent about their views on the appropriate distribution of economic resources. Unless the data necessary to know what is occurring is made available, and unless politicians are forced to state their views on the distribution of economic resources, there is no method of integrating individual preferences into the social-welfare function.

If the political process cannot be reformed to make the evaluation of social priorities more open, there is little sense in analyzing the impact of taxes on the American economy. It is analogous to calling in a technician to tell you whether your mechanical street-sweeper is working efficiently. He carefully examines the machinery, pronounces it in working order, but does not look up to see whether the sweeper is sweeping the right street. If the machine is consistently on the wrong streets, the technical efficiency of the machinery is irrelevant. In a similar manner if the tax system starts with an inappropriate social-welfare function, its technical efficiency is irrelevant. Moreover, such inefficiencies contaminate the entire economy. If a private market economy starts with an inappropriate distribution of economic resources, it is also inefficient in the large regardless of how efficient it is in the small.

Thus a reformulation of the process by which Americans make social-welfare judgments in the area of taxation is a first priority. Reform should start with some mechanism for more widely publicizing the existing distributions of economic resources and for inducing political candidates to reveal how they think the existing distributions should be modified. To insure that the public knows what is occurring it is also necessary to implement a requirement that tax laws be written in such a fashion that nominal and effective rates can not differ by other than trivial amounts.

The Appropriate Tax Bases and Rates

Americans seem to be interested in the distribution of consumption, human capital, and physical wealth. All of these items are to some extent now taxed, and there probably would be a popular outcry if the government were to announce that it is no longer interested in the dispersions in consumption, earned income, or wealth. At the same time there isn't much interest in seeking some indirect method of taxing leisure (such as high taxes on goods that are complementary with leisure).

Given the intent of the currently ineffective inheritance laws and the equal opportunity laws, society seems to be interested in the process by which individual locations are determined in the distribution of economic resources as well as the shapes of the distribution itself. Individual positions are expected to be random with respect to race, religion, color, creed, and family background, but nonrandom with respect to individual ability and initiative. Those at the top of the distribution are supposed to have earned their positions at the top.

With the exceptions of eliminating the impact of family wealth through inheritance laws, taxation is not a technique for insuring that the processes for determining individual positions on the distribution of economic resources are just. This is the goal of other public policy instruments, such as educational policies, housing policies, training policies, and so forth. Taxation is simply the instrument for altering the overall shapes of the distribution. It cannot move individuals to specific positions.

But what shape of distribution does society wish to achieve? Given preferences that everyone earns his own living, there is some minimum quantity of human capital that each individual should possess. This means that society wishes to eliminate the lower tail in the current distribution of human capital. Taxation cannot do this alone, but it can contribute by eliminating earned income taxes on those whose human capital (earned income) is below the prescribed limits. The 1969 tax reform law in fact took a step in this direction.

The Family Assistance Plan of President Nixon (the negative income tax by another name) is also a step in the direction of eliminating low family incomes regardless of their source. The purpose of such a step is to set a minimum consumption floor for any family. Thus society also seems to be interested in eliminating the lower tail of the consumption distribution. This presumably means consumption (sales) taxes should be eliminated for low-consumption families or that negative income taxes should be set to allow for the additional expenses of paying sales taxes on consumption goods.

While the effective tax rates in the Federal personal income tax are much less progressive than the nominal rates, excess burdens make the effective tax rates more progressive than they would seem to be (*see* Chapters 1 and 4). Before-tax incomes would be much higher without taxes than they are with taxes. In all probability the American public wants a progressive tax structure, such as those in the nominal rates, but would like to eliminate excess burdens to provide a larger income for everyone. This means a systematic integration of consumption taxes and income taxes or consumption taxes and wealth taxes (*see* Chapter 7) to promote higher investment. Highly progressive consumption tax rates would thus be necessary.

Since present income taxes include unearned income, since property taxes are systematically collected in all jurisdictions, and since America has a nominally, if not effectively, stiff inheritance law, society presumably wants to tax wealth. Given the desired progressivity in income taxes and inheritance taxes, it presumably does not want the regressive tax structure that emerges with respect to physical wealth (*see* Chapter 4). Wealth tax rates should go up as wealth goes up, not down. To do this it is necessary to adopt a comprehensive system of wealth taxes that can be applied at progressive rates.

Theoretically, income taxes can be used to provide indirect controls over the distribution of wealth, but practical problems prevent their use for this purpose. Debates emerge about taxing unrealized gains, treating increases in wealth as income, and finding some method of taxing the consumption benefits of wealth generated by homes, paintings, and the like. In any case, using income taxes as indirect taxes on wealth violates the earlier axiom about keeping the system simple enough for the average citizen to express his preferences. Most individuals simply would not understand how income taxes could control the distribution of wealth.

Thus a comprehensive system of wealth taxes should be adopted as a replacement for the current income taxes on unearned income and property. All types of physical wealth would be assessed and taxed at some common but progressive rate. In all probability the rates would be more progressive than those in earned income. The tax would be levied at frequent intervals, but the interval need not be one year; it might be anything up to five years.

Since Americans seem to believe that an individual's position in the distribution of economic resources should depend upon his own efforts and not those of his ancestors, and since Americans are probably willing to let a man accumulate more wealth than they are willing to let him inherit, an inheritance tax would still be necessary to complement a wealth tax. Society is simply saying that its desired distribution of wealth varies depending upon whether that wealth is earned or inherited.

Inheritance taxes, however, need to be reconstructed to achieve these objectives. Instead of being levied on the giver or his estate, they should be levied on the recipient. The recipient would pay taxes based on his lifetime accumulation of gifts and inheritances from all sources. If society really believes its rhetoric that no one should start life with a substantial financial head start on the rest of the population the inheritance tax might be organized with two rates, zero and 100 percent. For example, an individual might be allowed to accumulate gifts and inheritances up to $100,000 ($100,000 places an individual in the top $2\frac{1}{2}$ percent of the current wealth distribution) without paying any taxes, but would then be forced to pay a 100 percent tax after this point.

The existing structure of fiscal federalism fails to meet any of the demands that should be placed upon it. It does not finance minimum quantities of merit wants for all of its citizens, it does not handle the problem of externalities, it does not solve the problem of local resource inequalities, and it creates both horizontal and vertical inequities (*see* Chapter 6). Recent discussion of the solutions to these problems has revolved around different programs of unrestricted grants from the Federal government to state and local governments. Such systems are inadequate since they can potentially solve only one – resource inequalities – of the four basic problems in fiscal federalism. In addition, they are politically naïve in that they expect one group of politicians – the president and U.S. congressmen and senators – to take all of the political blame for raising taxes and then give the revenue to another group of politicians – state and local governors, mayors, etc. – so that the second group can claim the credit for the expenditures and for solving society's problems. Although token systems of this sort might be proposed (President Nixon did so in 1970), they are not apt to become large enough to provide the desired degree of equalization in the provision of public services. As a result, the only answer is some set of piggyback taxes under which there is one tax structure, but each state and locality sets its own tax surcharge that must be added to the Federal tax rate in its own area. Local citizens would pay taxes based on their local surcharges, but local revenue yields would depend upon what local tax surcharges would yield if the local area had the average, rather than its actual, quantity of economic resources. In this manner there could be resource equalization while preserving local taxation. Such a system is also necessary if national standards of vertical or horizontal equity are to be achieved. It is simply impossible to construct one Federal tax system that can counterbalance thousands of different local tax systems.

Even with piggyback taxes, however, it would be necessary to have Federal grants-in-aid for financing minimum quantities of merit wants (project grants) and matching grants for goods with externalities. These types of grants, however, now exist and are accepted. They also give the political credit for projects to those politicians who take the political blame for raising the necessary taxes.

An ideal system of taxes would thus be composed of an earned income tax, a consumption or expenditure tax, a comprehensive tax on physical wealth, and a piggyback tax structure for state and local governments. For both earned income and consumption there would be some quantity of earnings and consumption that would be untaxed. These would correspond to whatever society sets as its long-run minimum standards of living. (I opt for setting such a line at 50 percent of the median standard of living, but this is another problem.) Above the zero tax bracket, the rate structure would be progressive for both consumption and earned income.

Given a desire to prevent excess burdens, the consumption tax rate structure would need to be more progressive than that for earned income. At the same time American preferences seem to lead to wealth taxes that are more progressive than earned income taxes. Since progressivity in consumption taxes must also exceed that in wealth taxes to reduce excess burdens, the desired degree of progressivity in wealth taxes would to some extent dictate the necessary degree of progressivity in consumption taxes.

Each state and local government would set a tax surcharge but not the tax structure for its regions. The revenue produced by these tax rates, however, would be based on the average distribution of economic resources rather than local distribution. Matching grants and specific block grants-in-aid would be set to handle the special problems of goods with externalities and merit wants.

Inheritance taxes would be levied on the recipients and at a progressive rate structure that would reflect society's tolerance for allowing individuals to have a financial head start on their fellow citizens. Based on American rhetoric the allowable head start would be small.

Macroeconomic Policies

Alternative taxes differ substantially in terms of both the magnitude of their impact on the aggregate demand and supply of goods and services and upon the timing of that impact (*see* Chapter 5). At one end of the spectrum corporate income taxes act relatively slowly, while at the other end of the spectrum personal income taxes act quickly. In terms of bringing the economy to full employment, personal income taxes are 30 percent more effective dollar for dollar, but corporate income taxes can be used to influence the supply as well as the demand for goods and services, while personal income taxes can only be used to affect the demand for goods and services.

In terms of affecting the distribution of economic resources, macroeconomic effects dominate all others. Every 1 percentage point deviation from society's unemployment target reduces the Gross National Product by approximately 3 percent. At 1970 output levels this means losses of $30 billion per year. As costly as this may be, the losses are also not spread equally across the population. They tend to be concentrated on those who suffer from unemployment and reductions in hours of work during recessionary periods. This means those at the lower end of the income distribution. Since the inflation that accompanies low unemployment also serves to equalize the distribution of income, the macroeconomic distributional impacts of taxes are substantial.

As a result, if society desires more equality in its distribution of income, it should set its tax policies to obtain full employment. It may decide that the costs of inflation in terms of horizontal inequalities outweigh the benefits in terms of vertical equalization, but this should lead to the construction of alternative policy instruments for controlling inflation, such as wage-price guideposts, not deliberate increases in unemployment. There is no doubt that the indirect inequalities created by excessive unemployment are much more extensive than any direct equalization of economic resources produced by the current tax system (*see* Chapter 4).

Microeconomic Policies

Although taxes are necessary to achieve social balance, they also make it impossible to achieve social balance in a private market economy. Individuals will not invest enough to bring the social rate of return on investment into equilibrium with the social rate of time preference. To some extent, however, highly progressive consumption taxes reduce this problem.[1] Consumption becomes a less attractive alternative to investment. The remaining part of the problem must simply be accepted as one of the necessary costs of a market economy. Presumably in the views of most Americans it is more than offset by the benefits of such a system.

In theory the negative excess burdens produced by increased work effort on the part of labor could cause just as great a reduction in social welfare as the positive excess burdens produced by less investment. Perhaps it is our Puritan background, but it also may be that as a society we are much more worried about reduced investment than we are about increased work effort. As a result it is not necessary to design a tax system that eliminates these negative excess burdens. If such a system were desired, however, it presumably could be achieved through increasing the progressivity of the tax on earned income.

The positive excess burdens of the tax system are produced by the impact of taxes on investment decisions rather than savings-consumption decisions. Thus the problem is one of removing the disincentives to investment rather than removing the disincentives to savings. If the tax structure were set to encourage more investment, however, accommodating changes would need to take place in the current structure of macro-economic policies. In all probability, some of the necessary savings would need to occur in the form of public savings (budget surpluses), but this might not be necessary if a progressive structure of consumption taxes were adopted.

As the system now stands, taxes do not substantially reduce society's savings since the propensity of governments to save and invest is approximately the same as private propensities to save and invest. Using a bricks-and-mortar definition of savings, individuals save slightly more than governments, but using a wider definition of savings that includes human capital investment, governments save slightly more than individuals (*see* Chapter 2). Assuming efficient investment decisions on the part of private individuals and public agencies, the approximate equality in savings rates might be taken to indicate that benefits from current private and public consumption are in balance with the benefits from future private and public consumption. The returns from future private and public consumption have been driven down to the social and private rate of time preference.

Given the pattern of consumption income and price elasticities used in Chapter 3, existing sales taxes do not seem to exert a great distorting effect on the pattern of consumption expenditures. The largest effect may come in the consumption of owner-occupied housing, but this is an area in which a number of government programs (including the tax deductibility of mortgage interest payments) work in the opposite direction. As a consequence the reliance of local governments on a wealth tax that only includes property produces both horizontal and vertical inequities, but it is not the prime cause of housing shortages. Land, interest, and construction costs are more to blame.

International consumption patterns may be more affected. If the European countries rely on rebatable value added taxes, while America relies on the nonrebatable corporation income, American investments in exports (and import substitutes) will be reduced relative to European investments. This might be offset, however, if Europeans had higher taxes on wealth, unrealized capital gains, or realized capital gains. In any case such tax induced shifts will be reflected in and offset by the structure of exchange rates, tariffs, and quotas. Thus there may be a slight reduction in the American standard of living, but reliance on corporation income taxes probably does not cause major alterations in the balance of payments. In the intermediate run everyone's balance of payments must balance.

Responses

Many individuals would argue that any stress on eliminating the excess burdens of taxation is inappropriate. America is so rich that it should not worry about expanding output or reductions in output caused by taxes. There are several counterarguments. First, I believe that it is inappropriate for anyone to call for a halt in economic growth unless he himself resides in the lower half of the income distribution or is willing to tax himself so that he has the same income as these families now have. Second, although American preferences seem to indicate an interest in raising the incomes of the poor and perhaps equalizing the income distributions for whites and blacks, Americans do not seem willing to do this at the expense of lowering families' existing standards of living. This means the resources for equalization must come from economic growth and a larger Gross National Product. We could equalize economic resources without growth, but we are not willing to do so. Third, economic growth is the only technique for maintaining full employment in a market economy. Without it we not only stop equalizing incomes, we make them more unequal.

Another response to this chapter will be to argue that according to the doctrine of revealed preferences society wishes to do whatever it does do. Thus the present tax structure is society's desired tax structure and its optimum tax structure since it has been set in the political arena. There are also several responses to this argument. First, it means that the political system works perfectly, and society never makes mistakes. Both propositions are difficult to believe. Second, it assumes that society knows all of the impacts of its tax decisions. If this were true, books of this sort would be needless repetition of existing knowledge. Perhaps it is professional egotism, but I suspect that at least potentially such is not the case.

Conclusions

Tax decisions are probably society's most important economic decisions since they determine the division of resources between public and private goods and the distribution of private resources among different families and individuals. In addition they strongly influence the distribution of resources between future consumption (investment) and current consumption. It is difficult to think of other economic decisions that are of comparable importance.

Based on the analysis of the first eight chapters and the implications drawn here, the American tax system is in need of substantial revision. Recent tax-reform measures have concentrated on the legitimacy or illegitimacy of this or that loophole. Although such reforms are needed if the current tax structure is to be made more equitable, the current tax structure needs a fundamental reorganization. At present, it is incapable of performing the necessary functions. The essence of such a reformulation would·be the adoption of a comprehensive system of wealth and inheritance taxes and the development of an integrated system of federal, state, and local taxation. Such a reform would be a major step toward achieving a more equitable social balance.

Note

1. For a rigorous discussion of what would be necessary to come as close as possible to solve this problem theoretically *see* W. J. Baumol and D. F. Bradford, "Optimal Departures from Marginal Cost Pricing"; A. P. Lerner, "Optimal Taxes with an Untaxable Sector"; and A. K. Dixit "On the Optimum Structure of Commodity Taxes," all in the *American Economic Review* (June 1970).

Appendix: Distributions of Net Worth

Whenever possible, taxes were assigned to specific types of capital assets (for the actual distribution of capital assets by size of net worth and income, see Table A-1). Thus, the corporation income tax was assumed to affect the value of stocks, the property tax was assumed to affect the value of property, the household's "own home" and "other investment assets"; motor vehicle taxes were assumed to affect the value of the household's "automobile." Personal taxes were split between taxes on labor earnings and taxes on capital earnings. That part of personal taxes on capital earnings was split into taxes on business and professional capital income, dividends, rents, and interest payments. These tax payments were then spread across the different net-worth classes based on an effective personal tax rate that was calculated from the cross-distribution of income and net worth. In the case of business and professional net worth, net worth was assumed to be dependent upon the after-tax labor earnings of the owners as well as the after-tax capital earnings. Consequently, labor taxes were assumed to affect business and professional net worth.

Since changes in the capital stock, excess burdens, are included in the calculations, eliminating taxes on stocks and on businesses and professions increases net worth in these areas beyond a simple capitalization of tax payments. Individuals invest more and expand the capital stock. Thus, Table A-2 is an estimate of net worth after these adjustments in the capital stock have been made.

Appendix

Composition of Net Worth, December, 31, 1962: Mean Amount of
Grouped by Size of Net

Group Characteristic	Total Net Worth	Tangible Assets			Business, Profession (Farm and Nonfarm)	Life Insurance, Annuities, Retirement Plans
		All	Own Home	Auto-mobile		
All Families	22,588	6,612	5,975	637	3,913	1,376
Size of Net Worth:						
Negative	−538	121	37	84	92	67
0–$999	302	214	72	141	30	124
$1,000–4,999	2,809	1,706	1,284	422	127	563
$5,000–9,999	7,305	4,536	3,996	540	404	927
$10,000–24,999	16,281	9,422	8,634	789	1,656	1,511
$25,000–49,999	35,309	14,956	13,721	1,236	5,283	2,625
$50,000–99,999	67,042	15,748	14,429	1,319	15,701	4,342
$100,000–199,999	129,958	26,960	25,215	1,745	22,484	5,312
$200,000–499,999	293,655	27,209	24,691	2,519	65,832	8,803
$500,000 and over	1,176,281	54,006	51,452	2,554	248,811	18,677
1962 Income:						
0–$2,999	8,875	3,901	3,752	149	1,418	190
$3,000–4,999	10,914	3,956	3,544	412	1,902	635
$5,000–7,499	15,112	5,615	4,973	643	2,050	1,135
$7,500–9,999	21,243	8,367	7,499	868	2,577	1,879
$10,000–14,999	30,389	10,873	9,527	1,346	5,174	2,975
$15,000–24,999	74,329	17,004	15,188	1,816	9,088	5,196
$25,000–49,999	267,996	35,090	32,215	2,875	66,144	10,819
$50,000–99,999	789,582	48,764	45,961	2,803	251,977	19,559
$100,000 and over	1,554,152	89,645	85,634	4,011	288,915	32,309
Age of Family Head:						
Under 25	762	544	248	297	36	125
25–34	7,661	2,798	2,300	498	1,014	678
35–44	19,442	5,952	5,244	708	3,939	1,496
45–54	25,459	8,557	7,645	912	5,776	2,241
55–64	34,781	9,206	8,465	741	6,275	1,789
65 and over	30,718	7,846	7,474	372	3,267	873

[1]Board of Governors of Federal Reserve System, "Survey of Financial

A-1[1]
Specified Assets or Debt Held by All Families in Group — Families
Worth, Income, etc. (dollars)

| | | Liquid and Investment Assets | | | | | Less: Personal Debt (Excludes Auto) |
| | | | Investment Assets | | | Miscellaneous Assets | |
All	Liquid Assets	All	Stocks	Marketable Bonds	Other		
9,642	2,579	7,063	4,072	456	2,535	1,528	483
82	64	18	7	1	10	3	903
108	98	11	1	2	8	13	186
731	631	100	46	4	50	76	394
1,655	1,268	397	150	8	240	197	374
3,980	2,266	1,715	567	8	1,140	241	529
11,874	5,961	5,914	2,132	272	3,510	795	225
30,560	9,512	21,048	9,659	461	10,928	1,181	490
73,068	14,454	58,614	38,301	2,202	18,111	3,795	1,662
182,006	19,151	162,855	105,160	4,249	53,445	11,464	1,659
590,160	40,973	549,187	363,208	79,023	106,956	273,272	8,646
3,458	1,330	2,128	1,480	201	448	113	205
4,663	1,738	2,925	818	19	2,088	137	378
5,426	1,716	3,710	2,365	18	1,326	1,339	453
7,500	2,722	4,779	1,476	44	3,258	1,632	712
11,202	4,233	6,969	3,761	316	2,893	749	584
39,880	9,241	30,638	18,733	1,445	10,460	3,664	502
111,761	19,098	92,663	58,111	4,742	29,810	48,736	4,553
387,573	41,845	345,728	204,665	71,971	69,092	86,313	4,604
1,058,672	54,426	1,004,246	758,253	121,985	124,008	96,879	12,268
381	256	125	44	(1)	81	169	493
1,566	647	919	515	29	375	2,098	492
6,061	1,566	4,505	2,356	195	1,953	2,541	546
8,144	2,563	5,581	2,834	272	2,475	1,472	730
16,647	4,117	12,530	7,542	695	4,293	1,220	356
18,452	4,670	13,782	8,349	1,234	4,198	535	256

Characteristics," *Federal Reserve Bulletin* (March 1964), p. 293.

TABLE A-2[1]

Estimated Composition of Net Worth Without Taxes

Row	Size of Net Worth	Tangible Assets				Business Profession	Life Insurance Annuities Pensions
		Total Net Worth	All	Own Home	Auto- mobile		
	(1)	(2)	(3)	(4)	(5)	(6)	(7)
1	Negative	−514	139	51	88	92	67
2	$0–999	340	246	99	147	30	174
3	1,000–4,999	3,372	2,210	1,769	441	128	563
4	5,000–9,999	9,146	6,071	5,506	565	416	927
5	10,000–24,999	20,760	12,723	11,098	825	1,755	1,511
6	25,000–49,999	44,874	20,201	18,908	1,293	5,732	2,625
7	50,000–99,999	87,942	21,263	19,883	1,380	17,240	4,342
8	100,000–199,999	181,096	36,571	34,746	1,825	24,935	5,312
9	200,000–499,999	426,483	36,659	34,024	2,635	75,048	8,803
10	500,000 and over	1,615,250	73,572	70,901	2,671	294,592	18,677

[1]Calculated from Production function Analysis presented in Chapter 4 and data from Table A-1.

TABLE A-2 (*cont.*)

Row	Liquid and Investment Assets						Miscel- laneous Assets	Less Personal Debt
	All	Liquid Assets	Investment Assets					
			All	Stocks	Marketable Bonds	Other		
(1)	(8)	(9)	(10)	(11)	(12)	(13)	(14)	(15)
1	88	64	22	7	1	14	3	903
2	113	98	15	2	2	11	13	186
3	789	638	151	77	4	70	76	394
4	1,909	1,305	604	254	8	342	197	374
5	5,059	2,402	2,657	969	8	1,680	241	529
6	15,746	6,468	9,278	3,669	295	5,314	795	225
7	44,406	10,444	33,962	16,681	506	16,775	1,181	490
8	112,955	16,029	96,926	66,376	2,442	28,108	3,795	1,662
9	296,168	21,832	274,336	183,820	4,844	85,672	11,464	1,659
10	963,783	48,512	915,271	642,878	93,563	178,830	273,272	8,646

Index